Thank you for your love & — Challenge your belief often

PROSPERITY CODES

HOW TO ATTUNE TO & ATTRACT WEALTH, JOY AND ABUNDANCE

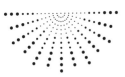

Love, Rorri

ALYSEMARIE GALLAGHER WARREN   ANDREA BLINDT

BRIGID HOLDER   DONNA MICHELLE WREN

JOCELYN CHONG   KA KI LEE   KERRI SCOTT

LISA LORNA BLAIR   MARDALENA DAWN TURPEL

MARY GOODEN   SARA GAROFALO   SHIRLEY JOFFE

TRACEY RAMPLING BROWN   TRICIA MCKENNA

EXALTED PUBLISHING HOUSE

Disclaimer

The publisher takes no legal responsibility for the details inside the stories of this book. The words and opinions are the writer's own, the memories they describe are their lived experience and I do not have any evidence that those stories are untrue. I've chosen to trust the authors and have not done them the disservice of fact-checking every version of events. Memoirs are stories from one person's vantage point and these experiences are unfortunately, universal and this is why we've chosen to share them in this collection.

Although the publisher and the authors have made every effort to ensure that the information in this book was correct at press time and while this publication is designed to provide accurate information in regard to the subject matter covered, the publisher and the authors assume no responsibility for errors, inaccuracies, omissions, or any other consistencies herein and hereby disclaim any liability to any party for any loss, damage, or disruption caused by errors or omissions, whether such errors or omissions results from negligence, accident, or any other cause.

CONTENTS

INTRODUCTION

Webster's dictionary defines *prosperity* as "the state of being prosperous."

The first thought, "Ok, well what does that *truly* mean?"

And *prosperous*: (adj.) as "having success; flourishing. Well-to-do; well-off. Propitious; favorable."

Again, sounds quite ambiguous to most.

Because how can prosperity really be understood by the definitions above if not in a relatable context.

Prosperity is not a one-size-fits-all potion. It's not something that you can bottle up for one person and say this is the end-all-be-all for another. That's the magic of it, really.

The stories that you will read in this book meander through life experience, background, upbringing, jobs, careers, values and beliefs. The women each bring an unparalleled definition and understanding of abundance, prosperity, joy and wealth to the table.

What we have come to acknowledge and realize is that everyone has their own unique "prosperity code". What is right for one, leaves something to be desired for another.

Some people want gold necklaces, the latest Chanel purse and the newest iPhone.

Some desire organic food at their fingertips, money flowing from doing that in which they love and close-knit relationships.

Some want the $200k per year salaries, the nicest cars, the first class flight experience and the luxury apartment.

Some desire something more elusive; a feeling or a state of being related to their own definition of prosperity.

Who is to say what is right or what is wrong in the eyes of *prosperity*?

No one.

We each have the ability to define what is true and right for us and lead our lives as a shining example of our own values.

Allow each chapter to serve as an opportunity for self-reflection. Each woman brings forth her own unique expression of what prosperity, joy, and abundance look like in her life. She is able to share openly through her story, words, beliefs, challenges and miracles and show you what prosperity looks like, feels like and maybe even tastes like to her.

Enjoy each moment as you read and cheers to *you* finding your way to your own, "Prosperity Code."

1

ALYSEMARIE GALLAGHER WARREN

THE HOUSE OF PROSPERITY IS BUILT OUT OF LOVE

I'M GOING to start with a big vulnerable share, mostly because I need to put it down on paper and get the words out of my head: I don't feel like I belong here. I don't believe I have any business sharing with you about prosperity. I don't feel qualified to help you re-code your relationship with wealth and money.

I began writing this chapter with many doubts and fears, and all the little voices in my head telling me I'm a fraud. And yet, I showed up. I came here guided by Mary Magdalene who is ready for me – and for all of us – to shed our limited ideas and scope of what being wealthy, prosperous, and rich means for our lives.

There, I said it. I am 100% honest. I'm walking this journey with you. I haven't made it. I haven't found the secret. I'm at the beginning just like you, and this chapter is a huge, very important step, diving deep into the medicine of our lives.

Medicine, you ask. What do you mean? When I say medicine in this sense, I am trying to evoke a spoonful-of- sugar-makes-the-medicine-go-down vibe. But I am also talking about the nuggets of wisdom that are presented to us, that help us to heal, move forward, or understand. While I'm explaining things, let me also talk about codes. Codes are bits of ingrained memories, lessons, ideas, wisdom, or understandings. In my mind, codes work a little bit like The Matrix. You get tapped in and for unexplained reasons, things just begin to make sense. Every cell in our body has codes, like DNA that just explain to them how to be. Wealth or prosperity codes work much in the same way.

I also need you to know that there was a time before money and jobs and the masculine structure of wealth, when everyone felt tapped into this idea of prosperity. This is what we are striving to get back to: the open flow of energetic wealth and the fountain of prosperity that is free to all.

So, here we go.

Let's examine my life and explore some ways that prosperity has shown up quietly, that I never allowed myself to recognize. All the times I overlooked things to keep myself small, kept myself feeling inadequate to fit in, or to maintain the status quo. I told myself I was lucky instead of prosperous. I never considered that prosperity could be rewarding me for all my hard work.

Our lives, our memories, our past...this is our medicine. When you have a memory pop into your head, it's offering you the medicine of that moment. It's showing up to be healed, or released, or to heal you. So often we dismiss these memories as tricks of the mind, and we miss the medicine of the moment.

I'll be taking you on a memory journey through moments in my life where the medicine of prosperity lives and is ready to be accessed. I invite you to do the same thing as you read this chapter. Let Mary Magdalene guide you through your life as well. Be a witness, take notes, allow all memories that surface for you as you walk my journey with me. You're not here by accident so let this memory medicine flow through you. This is an active meditation of your life, of your own prosperity, of the wealth that is your birthright.

My first memory, the place Mary has brought me to every time I begin to think about this book, is my childhood home. A house quite literally built of love: its journey was a labor of love. Instead of allowing the house to be demolished, we bought it for a dollar. We moved it across the street on giant rollers, rehabbed bit by bit, and restored it to its former glory. I loved our house and it loved me right back. When I recall memories of this home, all are filled to the brim with love. I felt so alive and a deep soul wealth in those four walls. It wasn't just the energy of the house, but the love that my family filled it with. Love is the thread of prosperity that leads you to being truly wealthy in a fully embodied sense.

In recounting this memory, I heard a whisper, "the house of prosperity is built out of love." I knew I had tapped into something when I heard that. As I reflect on how this makes me feel as an adult, I see the threads of love that have been woven throughout my life and all the places that love has been the source of prosperity. So, I asked myself, "What has embodied love given you?" I invite you to ask yourself this too. Think about your first memories of this kind of love, how has it affected your life? Can you follow the threads? What power has love had in your life?

Love has always been my resting place. The place I come back to and the foundation for all I do. Love is my rainbow, forever leading me to, and connecting me to, my endless pot of gold, the riches of life, and the wellspring of joy. Love has always been the beginning, the middle, and the end. I could go on for hours about the love that was fostered and grown in our house, but we must keep moving forward.

As I breathe deeply into where Mary is pointing, I see myself once again inside our house as a young girl: age 6, long ringlets, a toothless smile, giant dimples, and adventurous blue eyes, sitting with our family friend and my fearless babysitter, Louie. Louie was a gentle man in his mid to late 70's with a round belly, a few hairs on his head, round wire-rimmed glasses, and a kind spirit. The afternoons we spent together often ended in fits of pure, joyful laughter.

One day, I had a loose tooth. I was bound and determined to get that tooth out, no matter the cost. So, because I could talk Louie into just about anything, we started the process of tooth removal. First, I ate an apple, and we laughed. Then we wiggled and wiggled and wiggled and still it didn't budge, so we laughed. Next, we tried tying a string to my tooth, tying the string to the door, and closing it. I felt a jerk, but still that tooth didn't budge. So, we giggled, and we dreamed up more ways to get that darn tooth out. We laughed about using pliers, throwing a baseball at my mouth, hitting it with a hammer, but...I don't even remember if we got the tooth out that day! In the end, that wasn't the important part. The important part was how Louie made me feel: joyful and full of life.

Do you remember when you first experienced pure joy? Can you live in that memory and feel the prosperity growing inside you? Can you feel yourself tapping into your birthright, knowing that the best things in life can't be bought? The best things in life must be felt and embodied. This wellspring of prosperity is where we are being led. Our wealth codes lie in the truest expression of our feelings.

We are meant to be happy. We are meant to have wealth...to be prosperous. We were designed with these codes already in us but somewhere along the way we started reprogramming and undoing the codes. We started believing the lies created in fear that have driven us further and further away for our pure embodied expression of emotion. The walls built of lies about wealth have shifted the codes in all of us, as a collective. If we go where we are led, we can find the threads that lead us back.

Now we have two threads: love and joy.

Next up, Mary is showing me my high school art classroom, my teacher, Mr. Siska, my art room bestie, Heather, and a giant canvas that became my first self portrait. My face, divided in quadrants: one hidden behind a mask, one like raw meat, one in darkness, and one as I actually look. Each one shows a different part of how I showed up in the world. It was on the canvas that I first truly learned to see myself, understand my intuition, and follow where it led me. It was in putting paint on that canvas that I began to transmute and move my own energy. I learned to put everything I was feeling into the painting, letting myself feel and move. Creation unlocked the door to my intuition, my knowing, and my belief in myself.

I believe intuition is the basis of all belief systems. Intuition is the connection of all creation and the backbone of all wealth codes. When we follow our intuition and believe in endless possibilities, we attune to our unique prosperity codes. Here, in our deep inner knowing we feel the frequency that we must align with to attract the abundant wealthy life that is waiting to be claimed.

What is your relationship with your intuition or inner knowing? Do you listen to the nudges from deep inside your belly? Do you follow where it leads? Do you align with your intuition? This was another thread that Mary is highlighting to lead us back to our wellspring. But it's not just the intuition, but the belief that comes from aligning with our intuition. If we believe we are meant to be wealthy even if it doesn't make sense, because we trust that everything will work out for us, we are still attuning to that which is meant to be ours.

As I sit here writing in the dark of a five-star hotel room with a pounding headache, I feel myself attuning to my codes. Mary is leading me to the hardest story for me to tell, the part of my journey that I've kept separate for so long. I realize I can no longer lead a double life. I realized I needed to merge the part of my life where I am an Executive Chef/Partner with the part where I am a High-Level Master Healer. The two must become one. Unifying the masculine and feminine parts of ourselves is an important lesson to learn. I don't attune to my wealth codes without both halves!

The story of the chef-half of AlyseMarie starts when I was young, maybe six years old. I was making soup with my mom and family on Christmas Eve. We were making what is still my favorite soup: a hearty tomato broth, seasoned with dried basil, ground beef, mirepoix, and barley. It tastes and smells like home. It is a simple recipe, and every ingredient is essential. I was tasked with cutting the onions. My grandfather hated onions. So, when he asked, "Are there any onions in the soup?" and my mom responded, "No" hoping we had cut them small enough that he wouldn't notice, I was surprised. I chimed in, beaming, "Yes, there are, I cut them myself!" My grandfather grimaced and pushed his soup away as everyone at the table looked at each other in disbelief. I was smart enough to remember my contribution, but too young to understand the implications. Mary is reminding me of this specific memory because it combines the disparate parts of my code: the love of cooking, the joy of innocence, and the intuition of my inner voice. The love of cooking led me to become a chef, to care deeply about the ingredients and infuse them with love.

My chef self is guided by my feminine energy, but I lean heavily into my masculine side. We are taught that you must work hard: 70+ hours of work per week and sometimes more. As a woman you are told you have to work even harder. Need hours covered? I got you. Need someone to come in early? Sure, no problem. To be honest, I started doing this without even being asked and then it became my normal. I feel like I'll always have something to prove, so I do more. On top of that, I'm fat. So, I work even harder to compensate. I make all the jokes about my body and feel shame about everything I put in my mouth. All of this makes me feel the need to work even harder. In this, many times I lost the love, I lacked the joy, and I stopped believing things would ever change. So, I sought a pilgrimage to rediscover my feminine guidance.

I realized that I had a deep-seated belief that cooking kept me from my purpose, from flowing. I believed that restaurant life led me deep into my masculine energy and far from the feminine parts I was willing to leave behind because of my bodily shame. However, as I type, I'm realizing that being a chef is what allowed me to live my purpose every single day, healing the collective, one plate at a time.

Mary is highlighting that I'm not just a chef, and this is the hardest part for me to say: I'm an executive chef and part owner in a growing restaurant group. Not long ago, I ran into a former chef at his Las Vegas restaurant, and he asked me what I was up to these days. All I said was, "I work in a restaurant". As we walked away my husband asked me why I said it like that, and I didn't have a good answer. Do I need to remind you or myself that I was already a partner, I'd already been running my own kitchen! I told myself I was being shy, but honestly, I was playing small because my expansiveness has always scared people…and so I let it scare me too.

My bottomless pot of gold at the end of the rainbow, scares me. Because we have been so deeply coded with fear about wealth, we've been tricked. We've been lied to over and over again. We've been told that money is the only thing that makes you wealthy, abundant, and/or prosperous.

But, to come full circle, we have forgotten that there was a time before money existed. A time when the feminine and masculine lived in harmony…when we were deeply attuned to our bodies. A time when we believed that we could rise together…a time when we acted out of love, believing that living in a state of joy was the only way.

Mary is bringing me into this now, right here in this moment. She is encouraging me to spend a bit of time acknowledging where I am and showing up for you as my fully embodied self, to witness my accomplishments. This is another thread of the journey: seeing our prosperity, our abundance, our wealth in this very moment.

I am currently writing these words in my third co-authored book and my first two books were international best sellers. In the recesses of my brain I am simultaneously writing the words to another book and a column for an online magazine. At the same time, I am running a kitchen, creating my healing business, living and loving in a thriving marriage, and creating a deep connection with Mary Magdalene as she helps me create space and accept what is being asked of me. I am showing up and changing the vibration of the world. My path is a constant reminder that we can have the life we desire, one step at a time. The final thread is seeing, honoring, and acknowledging the success.

Do you accept and acknowledge your success? Is success a comfortable place for you? Do you share it with others? Do you celebrate? Do you give your success gratitude? This is a thread of prosperity that we must weave into our lives to truly embody and hold the vibration of our wealth codes. It is in celebration and gratitude for what we have that we attune to and open the door to fully receive our abundance.

While setting up everything to write this chapter, I scheduled a call with a mentor I truly admire The timing was divine as I was trying to find a way to close out this chapter and her words were exactly what I needed to hear. They went like this, "When you're doing so many things right, why are you focusing on the thing that feels like you're doing wrong?". That is the key: focus on the success that's already in your life, on the abundance you can see, on the prosperity you do have. The wealth already exists within you.

The prosperity key is ridding yourself of lack, fear, and playing small. It will not be easy, but it will be worth it. Let the love in, feel the joy, believe completely. Embrace your feminine and masculine energy and acknowledge your accomplishments. Weave the threads we explored, and you will be well on your way to re-coding your wealth. You will be living into the prosperity you already possess. Now, everything you desired is already yours because it all lives inside you.

Let intuition guide you.

Breathe and repeat.

Prosperity is built out of love.

Breathe.

Abundance is rooted in your belief.

Breathe.

Acknowledge and celebrate your success.

Breathe.

Everything lives inside you.

Breathe and receive.

In this moment you are attuning and aligning to your wealth codes.

Hand on heart...and breathe.

ABOUT THE AUTHOR

AlyseMarie Warren is a Master healer and the go-to "spiritual sidekick" for high level leaders. She helps high achieving women that have created 6 & 7 figure businesses to create safe spaces to rest, heal and process their success. AlyseMarie's work is rooted in her connection to Mary Magdalene to provide intuitive guidance while her connection to Mother Gaia allows her to be the grounded, spiritual confidant. AlyseMarie is an Executive Chef in Chicago and lives in a cute eclectic bungalow with her artist husband, Spence, and their cat Kramer.

Website: www.alysemariewarren.com

Instagram: @i.am.alysemarie

2

ANDREA BLINDT

WHEN YOU HAVE NOTHING YOU CAN CREATE ANYTHING

I IMAGINED prosperity to be the result of financial success, regardless of the quality of life I was experiencing. Wealth to me was defined by what I had. My net worth, the quantity of money in my bank account, my assets, and my ability to use them at any given moment without restriction, for anything I wanted or needed. I held that belief for the majority of my life, trusting that I could only get what I wanted in life by working hard for it. That understanding was engrained into my subconscious since I was born; the image of my single mom working to provide for my siblings and I was proof that hard work was required to survive. I worked tirelessly towards that destination, 'prosperity island' not yet knowing that living a prosperous life meant much more than having money or working hard to survive. Prosperity meant having abundance, ease, and fulfillment in life. I wanted to thrive. I craved happiness, and I was determined to create a life that was different than the one I had experienced growing up. In making that decision, I had to learn a new way of living and defining prosperity. I wasn't sure how life would look, but by taking a big leap, I allowed myself to explore what living a life of meaning and happiness could look like.

I started listening to myself and doing what felt right inside my body rather than listening to the direction of society. I changed career paths in the middle of college, leaving the field of teaching and entering into the world of nursing. I excelled academically, graduating at the top of my class in nursing school, and was chosen out of over a thousand applicants for a highly sought after position as a pediatric oncology nurse working at a prestigious hospital. I loved my job and pushed myself to constantly learn more, taking continuing education courses and becoming highly sought after in my profession. I worked hard, trusting that stability was my ticket to experiencing a prosperous life, and that finances would support me in creating the life I desired for myself and my family.

But money was only an illusion, a means that allowed me to inch closer to the things I believed would bring fulfillment, comfort, and joy in my life. I lived in that fantasy world, accumulating belongings and growing wealth until I was forced to learn that no amount of money could ever buy what I longed for or what I was about to lose.

I worked exhaustively allocating my earnings on purchasing organic food and paying for a top fertility doctor in order to help me conceive. Money vaporized from my account almost as quickly as it arrived, being spent on multiple fertility cycles that failed. I endured two miscarriages, multiple surgeries, and then after a complicated IVF cycle, I was pregnant with twins. I worked extra shifts during my pregnancy to save money for bills so that I could take time off with my babies to bond after their delivery. I excitedly stocked their nursery with all the gear I believed was essential and some frivolous things too. I was thriving in life and living what many would consider a successful existence. Everything was great until I was forced to deliver my twins prematurely.

My twins experienced complex medical challenges, and despite the medical advancements being made in the world, they were unable to be saved. Money could buy many things, it could prolong their lives, but it couldn't buy their health or future. The day my twins died I would have given my life's savings to have one more minute with them. Instead of spending money on what I wanted, which was a lifetime with them, I was paying for their cremations and funeral costs. Their medical bills continued to arrive in the mail for years after they died, adding insult to injury.

It took death for me to fully redefine what it meant to be prosperous in life and to fully step into abundance. Today, experiencing prosperity means I live life fully in health, in knowledge, and in limitless possibility. I am empowered knowing that I create my own abundance. And that, while the world might have a negative impact on it occasionally, I am the only one who gets to define what that impact means for me and how I choose to stand up and press forward despite it. Prosperity means I take control of my life and acknowledge that I am not a victim. I stand tall regardless of what is happening around me, because I know true wealth grows within me. I understand that I am capable of reaching my full potential by living an empowered life rather than a life with limits and restrictions. I stopped listening to my old beliefs and started creating new ones that inspired me and encouraged me to create a life worthy of passing on to my children.

I started by acknowledging that money could buy many things, but it could never buy the most important things. Some things are priceless. I learned that money isn't the only thing that brings value into life. More important than money for me was the way I felt, the connections I made, and the abundant life I could create simply by imagining it was possible. I learned that money can't buy happiness, because happiness is a feeling. Money could help me buy a car that I felt happy driving in, but the happiness that I experience from driving in that car is free, and it's available to anyone regardless of social status or finances.

I stopped working for money and started letting money work for me. I invested in myself, increasing my personal abundance and prosperity from the inside out. I stopped giving my power away to money, believing money could buy me the life of my dreams. Instead I started creating the life I wanted to live by taking daily actions that felt good in my mind and body, and eventually abundance showed up in my life.

Here are a few steps I took:

1. I chose to place value on purchasing natural cosmetics and healthy nutritious foods that are non-toxic and easy to digest. Money can support health, but it cannot create it. By investing in quality products I am using money as a resource that will strengthen my body.
2. Healthcare becomes wealth-care when we choose to invest in our physical and mental health regularly. I allow myself to spend time and money on creating balance in my life knowing that I am able to attract wealth when I make my health a priority. I spend money on therapists, massages, and a gym membership trusting that each time I choose to invest in myself, I am rewarded tenfold.
3. Health, happiness, and love are the true players in living a prosperous life full of abundance. They work together to create harmony and when prioritized, they often result in wealth. I saturate myself in experiences that allow me to feel happiness. When I am living a happy life, I am healthier and able to receive blessings more readily.
4. I understand that money can be a vessel that allows me to travel, explore, and experience the beauties of this world. I allow money to take me places I have dreamt of going, and I never allow a lack of money to stop me from finding a way. I know many people who have

traveled the world without money at all, and they have shared the most fascinating stories of beauty, community, and connection.

5. I know that money does not make me prosperous. The way I choose to live my life and the connections I create does.

6. I realize that money is often spent on things we don't see instant value in, but with clear intention and gratitude you can find the worth.

7. Meaningful relationships with intimate connections are priceless. I choose to spend time and money pouring into them knowing they will bear fruit.

8. I recognize that time is a gift, not an expense. I don't need money to give it, only a desire to share it.

9. I am now able to discern that money can be both a gift and a curse if we don't use it wisely and purposefully. Get curious about your thoughts around money and the meanings they have for you.

10. I believe that I live in an abundant world, trusting that there is enough money in the world for everyone. I know that my neighbor can be a millionaire and trust that there is enough money for me to become one too, if I desire.

11. The beliefs we have around money, prosperity, and abundance will shape our reality if we don't take the time to define them. By acknowledging the old beliefs my family held around money, I was better able to adjust them in a more empowering way that served me in life instead of limiting me.

12. When my family told me, "Money doesn't grow on trees", I reframed that story and pointed out the facts. Money really does grow on trees if you are willing to see it. When I open my eyes, I see orchards full of trees abundant with fruit ready to be harvested and sold. I see the ability that fruit has to bring health, new life, and healing. I understand that trees are commonly used in the creation of alternative medicine. In my world, having access to nature and knowing how to use it to improve the quality of my life, is far more valuable than money sitting in a bank.

13. I have changed the relationship I have with money. Leaving fear, lack, and uncertainty behind and leaning into trust, abundance, and acceptance.

14. I created new beliefs and mantras around money that keep my energy high and bring additional happiness into my life. When I receive money I smile and say confidently, "Money loves me", "People love to give me money", "I am a money magnet!"

15. I learned how to surrender and give thanks for what I have, instead of constantly looking past my blessings in search of more. I started asking for what I desire, and then I thank God for providing it,

knowing that it is already mine. I take inspired action, and then I let the details work themselves out.

Remember - in a world where we believe that money can buy anything, there are still limits. You can choose to spend money today on wellness, or later battling illness. You cannot change the past or the future, but you can give yourself a gift by living in the present.

After my twins died, I focused on self care. I spent years in therapy dissolving limiting beliefs and creating empowering ones. As I continued to heal my mind and body, I was able to successfully birth four more children, two without fertility treatments. I made a vision board and looked at it daily. I wrote affirmations on post-it notes and placed them on every wall in my house. I set alarms on my phone with reminders of how successful I was. I bought myself clothes that made me feel good and that looked great on me, and I started living the life I always wanted to live. It looked different than I had imagined when I first started out, but it is even better.

My desire for you is that you find immense value in the relationships you have and the memories you create. Remember prosperity first begins in your mind, and then it appears in your physical world. I encourage you to bravely envision your dream life and live today as though it is already here. You are worthy, you are capable, and it is possible to live an abundant life starting today.

ABOUT THE AUTHOR

Andrea Blindt is a registered nurse, holistic health practitioner, international best-selling author, and inspirational speaker who empowers others through her own personal healing journey. She helps her clients create wealth by amplifying their health. She supports patients as they discover ways to enhance prosperity in their lives by reclaiming their power; advocating for what is in their best interest, and learning the tools needed to be able to make decisions for themselves that are in alignment with their beliefs. This allows her patients to create abundance, experience tranquility, and live life with clear intention. Andrea has been featured on Natural Health Radio, Conceive IVF, multiple podcasts and publications, and is a contributing author for a parenting magazine. She lives in sunny California with her husband and four beautiful children. She loves being in nature, reading, and inspiring others to live their best life today.

Website: www.andreablindt.com

Instagram: www.instagram.com/andreablindt

Email: heal@andreablindt.com

3

BRIGID HOLDER

A LITTLE KNOWN SECRET ABOUT PROSPERITY: IT'S NOT ALL ABOUT THE MONEY (THOUGH IT HELPS)

PACK your carry-on bag because I'm going to take you on the wild journey of my adult life and show you how no matter what numbers you have in your bank accounts, prosperity is about life's riches.

For me, the thread that started it all was travel. I'm sure you've heard people say that travel is the only way you become wealthier while spending money? Well, that's an absolute truth.

Do you know how most people glaze over when you start talking about your overseas holidays? I was the opposite of that person when I was young. When friends or colleagues mentioned traveling, I peppered them with questions about what they saw, ate, experienced and felt. They happily shared memories while I devoured every word. I closed my eyes and imagined every detail.

I made mental and physical notes about the sights and places that sounded the most interesting, and before I knew it, I developed my own little travel bucket list. We didn't have Google back then, so I would go to bookstores and purchase books on places I planned to visit someday. Finally, in my twenties, I booked my first big overseas adventure—a three-month jaunt around Europe.

When I hopped on that first big jet plane, I felt prosperous. And proud. When I clicked that seatbelt in for the first time, it was like the signal at the starting line of a lifelong race I wanted to run. It never even occurred to me that I could have taken a friend or companion. Travelling alone is a joy, even today because it fills me up.

Of course, that first trip, a Top Deck European Tour, was the most I could afford at the time and probably one of the cheapest on the market. Still I felt like a Queen with my plans to spend the rest of my savings on activities and seeing sights. Being open and following this passion for exploration led me on a romantic train ride that would unfortunately, end in a wreck.

My bestie had family in England, so I stayed with them for a while. As I settled in, I met a young man, fell in love and got engaged. Little did I know that I would lose my love, my travel dream, and more, in just a couple of years. But in the grit, that's where the good stuff lives. I flew home to Australia and let him go with a broken heart that cuts to the soul.

Looking back, I'm grateful my English love affair went down in flames because it allowed me to be by my beloved Grandfather's side as he transitioned from this Earth. You may not know it at the time, but sometimes the Universe provides these moments that seem incredibly painful, but they are actually the greatest gifts. And you'll see that those gifts make for a prosperous existence. Of course, things were about to get much harder for me before I could see any of it.

To paint a picture of my relationship with my Grandfather, I must tell you that he was the man I loved the longest, at that point in my life. My Dad was in and out of the picture but my Grandfather, hands down my favourite person on Earth. He had a wicked sense of humour and a cheeky grin to match. As an adult, I understand his jokes better and I wish he were still around to share them.

My Grandfather loved his garden; he grew the tastiest strawberries and mandarins – the reason I planted fruit trees at my home recently was to remember him and receive his love – over 20 years since his passing. Nan would scold us for eating too much of his delicious fruit, even though he told us we could, but we never dobbed on him. He would just flash us a wink and a smile.

He was a wise man too. Once, we were in the strawberry patch, looking for the reddest, ripest ones, when he spotted a witchety grub (In Australia, these look like giant caterpillars, they are the larvae of moths) and suggested we eat it. Now let me tell you, these things are scary looking, and my first instinct was one of disgust. But he gently shared how the indigenous people of our lands in Australia taught him how they cooked and ate this food as they lived in harmony with nature.

Intrigued, I followed him and watched as he carefully cooked it. Now a piece of it was in my dirty hand and he told me, "it tastes like chicken." I trusted him. So in went the grub. It did not taste like chicken at all, but it wasn't too bad. This was an early lesson for me in opening my mind to new experiences. Our First Nations People loved and regarded this food, relying on it for nutrition. Society made me believe these things are gross or that we shouldn't do things like eat grubs or go after our weirdest dreams. This story is like a fine wine in that its significance evolves and deepens with me as I age. I'm 50 and only now do I fully understand the lesson Grandad taught me.

But there I was, a young woman in love on the other side of the world from her dreams. Back home in Australia after a whirlwind trip, I felt like I didn't fit into my old life anymore. Like outgrowing my comfiest pair of shoes. I had an inextinguishable itch to get back to Europe, to my fiancé, and so I threw myself into working to save money to get back there.

My career was progressing well and by all accounts, I was climbing the corporate ladder successfully at a young age. I worked as an Administration Manager for a large computer company. I had been there as a receptionist since I was 17 years old, and by age 22, I ran the administration team of seven while overseeing the warehouse operations alongside a colleague.

To advance my career, I took accounting classes at night but I didn't really care anymore. I wanted to live inside my romantic adventure. I started weekend shifts at the infamous Northies Hotel in Cronulla. My only splurge to date was a hot little red sports car, and even that was something I was willing to part with in exchange for my new life.

While saving every penny for my dream of marriage and Europe, I spent late nights on the phone with my fiancé for hours planning our life together. I hardly knew him, really, but that never occurred to me. We would have to spend the better part of a year in a long-distance relationship – not easy in the best of times let alone after a holiday romance.

My eldest brother burst my bubble when I shared my plans with him. Yes, I wanted to resign from my job, sell my car, get a working visa and buy a one-way ticket to Europe. What was wrong with that? I'll never forget his response and the lecture that followed.

I know now he was doing it to protect me when he asked me why I would leave this safe, comfortable life behind. He told me I should invest in a house and create a financial safety net for myself. He did not mean it harshly, but I did feel judged at the time. I know he wanted to be a father figure for me and right to suggest I think about the consequences. I thought he didn't understand me, my feelings or my dreams. I did consider his words, but I figured it was all based on his own belief system and conditioning. I wanted romance and adventure. To be an explorer of life! Of course, I went anyway.

Life has a sense of humour sometimes. I recently saw a white version of my fabulous, red car, the one I sold to move back to Europe. I was with my 13-year-old son at the time, I pointed out that I had the same car back in the day. I told him how I used to drive really fast over this little hill on my way to work so the car would catch air. Such a joy to watch the expression on his face change as he considered a cooler, younger version of his Mother.

After watching my red sportscar disappear with her new owner and a grip of cash in hand, I finally saved enough to back myself and get back to England. I journeyed around Europe, through Scotland, Wales and Ireland, before returning to live with my new man and work in England.

Life was just as I imagined. Weekend trips to France and Rome, working in jobs around the country. I'll never forget, as an au-pair for three young girls, 11, 8 and 3. The 3-year-old told me she hated me every day, the 11-year-old struggled thinking her mum did not love her, and the 8-year-old was a delightful enigma that brought me joy. This tiny human was as artistic, creative, and funny as any adult I've met before or since. Her older sister was smart, wise and courageous; the youngest was challenging and growing through losing her previous au-pair and taking it out on me. The drama was highly entertaining and I loved being with them. When they moved to Singapore, I was a better person for this experience, more prosperous again and then I officially settled in to live with my partner.

I started building a new life for myself and started a job back in the corporate world. Little did I know my finance, not as fulfilled as I was with my new life and adventure, would stray from me. My world crumbled when I found out, tears rolling down my face as I sat across from a friend reliving the moments he told me.

While working in a big company, I met one of the funniest women on the planet, and we are still friends today. On a fabulous trip to the south of France, we spent a week on the French Riviera. She did not mention the trip involved a 12-hour bus ride for fear I would pull the plug on the whole trip (and I would have). This is still one of the best holidays of my life, and I'm grateful to have been able to teach Pommy girls the Australian slang word for chicken (chook) while they cried with laughter. They taught me to apply fake tan. We danced and partied the nights away and I cherish those memories before my fiancé obliterated my world with his poor choices.

Lost and grief-stricken, I returned to Australia, hoping my family could help me heal. I didn't know what else to do. My broken heart would have to face another, even worse battle, as my beloved Grandfather fell ill.

I found myself in the hospital, knowing all too soon I would lose this man. I told him about how I wouldn't marry my first love and fiancé, about how much my heart hurt. From his bed, my Grandfather tried to lighten the mood a little and show me another life lesson as he said; "Well, I always knew you wouldn't marry him with that funny name. But you had a good time, right? It wasn't all bad and now you get to be here with us". Of course, he was right.

Tears roll down my face each and every time I recall this moment – I know how lucky I was for the events to unfold exactly as they did. A short sixteen days later, my beautiful, loving, stoic grandmother joined him, making good on her promise, "I will be with you soon, darling", just as she said. Despite the heart-shattering grief, it was a gift to be there with them on their most significant journey of life, their exit from it. I could get myself back to Europe any time, and I would. But this – this experience would certainly make me a richer person.

Experiencing such soul-crushing grief means that I was able to love with my whole heart. Every bit of that pain was worth knowing I went all in. My life would have been poorer had I not given myself fully to each of these experiences.

Life lurched forward as it does. To be sure I had made the right decision to call off my marriage, I returned to England for a short visit. In the end, that was the final twist of the knife but I'm glad I went. If only just to make 100% sure we were done. I left England for good and shortly after returning, I met my now husband of over 20 years.

When you are not seeking love, it's often delivered. Even when you swear-off men. Even when after you meet your life partner, and encourage him to date other women. I'm only glad my intuition took over long enough for me to give him my phone number.

I recall our first kiss in the driveway where our house now sits. To this day, I can still feel the passion and excitement of that moment. Still, I was recovering from many wounds, so I pushed and pushed him away. He lived 4 hours from where I lived in Sydney and 45 minutes from my hometown, which I frequented often. Ironically, I used distance as an excuse even after I did a long-distance relationship overseas.

Eventually, he had enough. He said, "you never make time to see me, even when you're in your hometown, so we should just move on. I am not here to be ignored". My spontaneity kicked in; I jumped into the car, drove the 45 minutes to his house and said, "OK, you got me – let's try this thing!" Within four months, I moved back to my hometown, something I had never imagined would happen.

Eight months after our marriage, we lost everything we owned in the house fire. I used to sleep naked, so I did not even have any underpants. What a massive lesson on material things. Could I have lived without that fire? Certainly. But did I take that big black cloud of smoke and find the silver lining? I sure did. That fire cleared the slate, the clutter, and junk and allowed us to reassess, realign and rebuild (both our lives and our home). Now, 16 years after the build, people still ask if our house is brand new.

My husband suffered a back injury at work and was laid up for almost a year. At the time, we were starting our new build so he was able to concentrate on that and ensure everything went to plan. He even picked up on a few crucial errors that would have cost us a lot of time and money. I don't believe in toxic positivity but I also don't believe in playing the victim. We are all worthy of something, even when we're suffering and going through the hard stuff. Life moves on around us and sometimes we need to move with it – which is so much more beneficial and efficient than fighting against it.

With the back injury, my husband found it difficult to work for someone else so he started his own business. I threw my full support behind him (including my bookkeeping skills). Now in our 18th year in business, we feel successful in many ways. Not only financially, but in our free and flexible lifestyle.

Within three years, we married, lost our home to a house fire, rebuilt and started talking about children. I went with it. Again the Universe had plans far beyond my own.

I did not plan on living in or near my hometown and starting a family while working as the General Manager of a national organisation. Nor did I realise that having two small boys join us would be the most difficult challenge I had faced in my life to date. I say it all the time, managing 15 women in the office and over 400 casuals in the field was easier than raising babies. Easier than getting your heart broken or losing a grandparent. As a Mother, you are given full responsibility for another human's wellbeing, feeding their little bodies and souls. Every single day I felt terrified I would stuff it all up. I faced my fears and did the very best job I could, and I would not change it for the world.

The boys are both teenagers now and bring many challenges as they grow into their bodies. I look at it as if they are adults under construction. My parenting coach says, "birthing a child does not give you power over them; it allows you the opportunity to practice sharing power". Never a truer word spoken, and it makes me recognise how blessed and prosperous I am to have these two young men in my life. I'm looking forward to the privilege of watching them take their own wild journeys through life.

Just a few short years ago I found publishing and started my own company creating a space for women to share their stories, their way. This in itself creates a prosperity beyond words for me – not feeling like you are going to work when going to work, is the best feeling in life!

These peaks and troughs of my life story, prosperity is not about wealth or money; it's about the fullness and richness in life, the experiences: the love and joy, the ups and downs. To me, prosperity looks like, risk, reward, love, loss, failure and doing it all again and again until our final exit. It is not all sunshine and rainbows; there are dark clouds and rain for days on the journey, but, oh boy! The stories we have to share because of all roller coaster rides are worth it.

ABOUT THE AUTHOR

7 x International Best-Selling Publisher and USA Today Best Selling Author Brigid Holder of The Art of Grace Publishing House, loves to push the boundaries of publishing. Her literary prose spotlights empowerment, truth telling, and women breaking barriers. She believes that stories have the power to impact and shift multi-generational patterns. Her goal, collaborate with others in leaving a legacy that evokes heartfelt wisdom, honours bad-ass hero-ine's, all the while cultivating a blazing literary trail for emerging authors to follow. Most recently, a new collaboration digital Magazine, The Journey of Words, is shining a light on all things writing and publishing for our entrepreneurial publishing industry. When she is not publishing, Brigid can be found hiking and at her boys sporting meets, fostering her own empowerment, and watching her family create lasting memories, surely to later be found bound by a curated collection of words.

Website: www.brigidholder.com

4

DONNA MICHELLE WREN

FEELING THE ENERGY OF PROSPERITY

Authors note:

It is my aim to show what prosperity is by creating pictures and evoking feelings, through words. I hope that my chapter inspires you to broaden your view on the energy of prosperity and abundance in your own life. Writing is a prosperous practice. It is an ongoing creation. It takes the abstract from our minds and hearts and alchemizes into words on a page, which incarnates again into different images and feelings by all who read them. If my chapter inspires you to write down all that you are grateful for and appreciate in your own life, then I am deeply humbled to have had this opportunity, and my purpose is made manifest.

EVERYTHING IS ENERGY. Literally everything. Whether it is something of matter that we can perceive through our 5 senses or something abstract like, for example, the feelings of; freedom, love, anger, fear, joy, boredom, hope and yes, prosperity. Each of these feelings is pure energy – it may be embodied in form such as; yelling and cursing (anger), smiling and laughter (joy), hugging and holding hands (love), sighing and laying on the couch (boredom) or having lots of money and material things (prosperity). For the purposes of this discussion, I would like to focus on the idea that the energy of prosperity is embodied in vastly more manifestations than simply money and material things. In fact, it is severely limiting the energy of prosperity and our experience of living a prosperous life to just think of it in those terms. Let's open the box. The small, confining box that centuries of industry, capitalism, and a power-driven, patriarchal society has thrown the energy of prosperity into and tried to keep out of our reach.

Prosperity is felt when we are thriving. And certainly, having a lot of money and material things can feel like thriving, in the context of living in a capitalistic society. But not all of us have material wealth, value it, or - here's the real truth - even for those who do have it, do not *feel* like they're thriving. Anthony Bourdain, Kate Spade, Kurt Cobain and Ernest Hemingway are just some of our most famous, and by capitalistic standards, most successful people with talent, recognition and material and financial achievement. Yet they took their own lives. These "prosperous" people *were not thriving in their inner lives*, although they thrived in the confines of the small, dusty box standards.

So, thriving, the *feeling* we experience when we are prosperous, must exceed the limits of money and material wealth. In fact, we can thrive and live a prosperous life whether or not we have great monetary or material wealth. I do believe however, that Maslow's, "Hierarchy of Needs" factors into this discussion, in that one must have their "Deficiency Needs" met before one can thrive, and feel prosperity in their life. I recognize, with deep empathy, that there are many millions of people all around the world who do not have this foundation.

I also believe that the energy of prosperity, that I will soon share with you, can be tiny seeds that anyone, no matter their circumstances, can plant in their life. And with time, and a commitment to planting more and more of these seeds, a person can grow a foundation of feeling prosperous - no matter their set point. For those of us who have a strong foundation whereby our basic needs are met, this is where our focus and nurturing of these tiny seeds of prosperity can grow, blossom and flourish into the most abundant and thriving life garden. However, no seed can grow without sunlight and water. Metaphorically, I offer you these two components in the form of appreciation and gratitude. It is not enough to notice the sunset, that's just step one – awareness. One must be grateful to witness its beauty and appreciate the magical qualities in the colors, the pace, the transformation, the gift of the sunset. This is how we feel prosperous. This is how we feel like we are thriving. The more we stop to feel grateful and deeply appreciate the beauty all around us, the more the seeds of prosperity will grow within us. It really is that simple. As the Law of Attraction would have it, one who cultivates this feeling of prosperity within them, as a dominant energy, will call into their lives more and more aspects that embody a thriving, prosperous manifestation. So, don't be surprised if the money and material wealth show up as well.

For now, though, let's open the box, actually let's throw out the box altogether. There is no containment for the energy of prosperity – it is as limitless as your imagination. For even during a difficult period of one's life, you can still choose to go within, and feel the gratitude and appreciation for all the beauty in your life, even if for just a moment or two.

Below, I have compiled a list of aspects that I feel an immense energy of prosperity and thriving, when I experience them in my life, and that list continues to grow daily. I have a journal where I write them down as I experience them, or soon thereafter. Abraham Hicks, Law of Attraction guru, would call this the List of Positive Aspects. Call it whatever you like, just do it. It solidifies your appreciation, your gratitude – it is the Miracle Grow for your seeds. And when you are having a tough day, you can open up your journal and simply read through what you have logged and I promise it will shift you, even if just a smidge, to a feeling of prosperity and abundance. I hope my list reminds you of the prosperity that is all around us. I hope while reading it, it brings a smile, a recognition, a feeling of prosperity within you. Mostly, I hope it inspires you to put the small, dusty box away, up on a high shelf and that you can open up to the prosperity within you and all around you. Maybe you will start your own list and maybe one day, you can share it with someone else. That is how the garden grows, thrives and prospers.

The energy of prosperity is felt…

Reaching for the juiciest peach off the tree in my garden, biting into the soft, fuzzy flesh, feeling the juice run down my chin.

Walking through a grove of cherry blossom trees in full bloom, whose sweet perfume fills the air as I sit under their soft, pink canopy.

Belly laughs with my best friend, tears are streaming down my cheeks and I can't catch my breath.

Lying on a soft blanket, in the grass, on a perfect Spring day, sun shining on my face, soft breeze in my hair and not a worry on my mind. Just peace in my heart.

My first sip of coffee every single morning. It never gets old.

Leaving my conscious mind in meditation, returning with a bolt of epiphany.

Taking a quiet shower after a hot, sandy day at the beach.

Weeding the garden. Digging in the dirt. Losing track of time and feeling deeply grounded with Mother Earth.

Hiking through a quiet, wooded trail, up a mountain, where I'm immersed in nature all around me. It is the buck I meet with eye to eye, for a few still moments, feeling his trust and curiosity before he takes off into the woods again. It is the melodious birdsong I hear as I continue on the trail until I begin to hear the sound of rushing water. It is the moment that I step into the clearing and witness a gushing waterfall, it's spraying water dancing with the sun's rays creating a rainbow.

Looking up at the moon and the star filled sky and feeling both tiny and insignificant, but also at one with the Universe, all at the same time.

Playing my singing bowls, guiding meditation and witnessing the peace it brings others.

My cats' private affection and purr that they reserve only for me.

Listening to my favorite song and dancing around the kitchen like no one is watching, because no one is.

Reading a page-turner on a Sunday afternoon, forgetting the world beyond my couch.

Creating art of any kind without any critical self-talk, just joy in the process.

Tasting sweet, rich chocolate as it melts in my mouth.

Breathing in lilac's sweet scent as I lay down in my garden.

My cats' playful craziness as they are wrestling and chasing each other around the house.

My house. Every aspect – the creaky, wood floors, the bumpy, old plaster walls, the 80 year old slate roof, the new windows that let in an abundance of sunlight, the fireplace where I create roaring, crackling fires to warm my heart and bones in the cold winter months. My small, serene meditation room, my children's messy bedrooms, my walk-in, girly closet, my plant filled bathroom, my own art and my kids' art on the walls. Photos of my daughters. A bowl of seashells we have collected from beaches near and far. My books. My kitchen counter where we eat and chat and laugh. The magnets on the fridge from places where we have traveled. My cats, laying in a sunny spot to sleep, even if it is the kitchen table. The neighborhood where we live, all of my friendly, kind neighbors. My ever-changing and growing garden. The huge, old father Oak tree in my backyard.

When my fever breaks after being sick for days.

My cat Remy, greeting me at the door and meowing, "hello" whenever I get home.

Driving around on a breezy, sunny day, with the windows open and my favorite songs blasting.

Sitting at the beach listening to the waves softly roll in and out, like a lullaby.

Hugs that last a little longer than I expected.

Waking up and opening my bedroom curtains to see everything outside covered in pristine, sparkling snow.

Watching the myriad of birds eat and play at my backyard feeders. The cardinal, in his showy red plumes, feeding off the ground, the tiny wrens perched on the fence, singing their hearts out, the black-capped chickadees, so dapper. The orchestra of their birdsong calms my nervous system.

Spending time with friends who are kind, open-hearted, supportive, funny as hell, spontaneous, deep, and authentic.

Every moment with my daughters, literally, all of the moments.

The scent of honeysuckle, so sweet I want to eat the tiny stamens.

Roses. Every kind. Every color. Every single rose.

Prosperity is also...

Healing from my PTSD, understanding my triggers and minimizing their impact.

Healing my inner child by giving myself the love she needed.

Knowing when I'm done - and ready to move on.

Learning how to create and uphold boundaries for myself.

Practicing self-discipline.

Setting a goal for myself and achieving it.

Hearing my fear voice, but not allowing it to influence me.

Healing from grief.

Not repeating my own dysfunctional patterns.

Learning how to do something new, well enough that I can teach it to others.

A healthy, supportive, reciprocal relationship.

Feeling gratitude, from the moment I wake in the morning, for another day in this precious human life.

Feeling appreciation for all that I am blessed with every night before I go to sleep.

Feeling joy and content with the simple beauty all around me.

Not a day goes by without me acknowledging the basics that I can so easily take for granted...

Heat in my living space in the winter.

Safe, clean drinking water.

Healthy foods to eat.

Closet full of clothing and shoes.

A place to call home.

My family and friends whom I love and who love me.

Sometimes prosperity is feeling safe again, feeling healthy again, feeling free again, feeling connection again. "Again" can feel like a super prosperous energy.

I pray that prosperity also looks like this to all people, everywhere...

Feeling safe to walk alone down any street – free from violence of any kind.

Feeling free and accepted about who you are and who you love.

Feeling safe and accepted in the color of your skin, your gender identity, your sexuality, your relationships, your religion, your workplace, your school, town, state, country.

While my list goes on and on, I hope I have captured for you, how I feel the energy of prosperity in my own life and that some of it resonates with you. I hope that my list opens you up to more possibilities of what the energy of prosperity can look like and how it is manifest all throughout our lives, in the small, quiet moments, the big, loud, colorful moments and everything in between.

It is my wish for us all to live in the energy of prosperity, deeply connected to the feelings of gratitude and appreciation in as many moments as possible - so much so, that we lose count.

Sending love to all,

Donna Michelle Wren

ABOUT THE AUTHOR

Donna Michelle founded Empowered Meditation & Sound Healing in 2018 during the most dynamic transition of her adult life. As a lifelong teacher and learner, she began an accelerated journey of divinely guided learning. Her new path began with coaching then meditation, yoga, Reiki and ultimately, sound healing. In these few years, Donna has worked with people of all ages and backgrounds, one-on-one, in small groups, large corporate, school groups and sports teams. She holistically combines all her training in each session as each person and group is beautifully unique. Through sharing her love and passion for meditation and sound healing and being witness to the peace it brings her clients, Donna is living her purpose.

Website: www.empoweredmy.com

Email: donna@empoweredmy.com

IG: @empoweredmeditation

FB: Empowered Meditation & Sound Healing with Donna Michelle

5

JOCELYN CHONG

888

"Gong. Hei. Fat. Choy." my Mum articulated each word.

"Gong Hei Fat Choy", my 3-year-old self-parroted back. On our way to visit family, a bag of fresh mandarins beside us, she was teaching me a series of Cantonese greetings.

Gong Hei Fat Choy - Wishing you happiness and prosperity.

Lung Tang Fu Joek - Wish you a prosperous and thriving New Year.

Sang Ji Hing Lung - Prosperous business.

Clearly, prosperity was a much-desired blessing. Even the 4 mandarins we would exchange alongside these greetings symbolized good luck and wealth.

And it wasn't limited to salutations.

Growing up in Malaysia, my world was filled with references to abundance and success. Holidays like Lunar New Year, and even Christmas, bore an invitation for fortune and expansion.

The numbers 8, 888 and 168 (numeric representations of prosperity in Cantonese) surrounded me. Phone numbers, car registration plates, you name it. These digits held prominence, even in the most mundane circumstances.

This fixation, this hankering, was so commonplace — so every day. Yet it never occurred to me to ask what prosperity would mean for me. *Have you ever wondered what it means for you?*

We all have a basic understanding of what being prosperous is. Usually tied to financial success and wealth, it's often associated with burgeoning material plentitude. That's certainly the concept I latched on to in my Accounting and Finance career.

But is that all it is? What if we took a more expansive view?

To me, **prosperity is the abundance, freedom <u>and</u> enduring fulfillment that comes with**

being true to yourself and living your purpose. Because the accumulation of wealth alone does not guarantee your happiness or satisfaction. And *true prosperity should uplift your soul.*

I learnt this the hard way.

Prosperity wasn't a term much-used in everyday vernacular when I first migrated to Australia in 1997. But as I progressed in my career as a financial advisor, I saw its connection to wealth acquisition and profitability, its links to luxury, success and security.

Using my expertise, I helped clients achieve financial freedom to live affluent lifestyles. I taught, educated, and empowered individuals and corporations to increase their net worth and secure their financial health. And I was good at it.

Very soon, I was climbing the corporate ladder, winning accolades and awards and being recognised as an industry leader. Yet despite every indication of success, prosperity seemed fleeting. An endless cycle of doing more, working more, buying more. All to ensure I was seen as prosperous.

I failed to see that working an average of 14-17 hours a day was unsustainable. I never questioned the interrupted weekends, the need to cancel on friends and family, or my inability to detach from my phone.

I had to be available 24/7. I had to measure up to the increasing demands put on me. Solve complex issues. Meet tight deadlines. Even if it meant I slept very little. Even if I felt like I was drowning in an endless sea of stress and tension.

The working conditions were fast-paced, intense and exhausting. But so what? This was the norm. My colleagues and competition all dealt with the same soul-crushing overwhelm and frustration. It was what it was, and I couldn't be the one to fall behind.

Besides, I was hooked. Addicted to the prestige of being an accomplished, in-demand career woman. Obsessed with the external validation of 'thriving', of winning.

And of course, I had to look the part. In an industry and network where prosperity was tied with material evidence of success, you were judged by the clothes you wore, the car you drove and where you went on holiday.

So I filled my wardrobe with high-end brands. Louis Vuitton, Prada, Salvatore Ferragamo and Gucci were my silent partners. Indicators of my eminence. I picked cars by their luxury factor and holidayed where my bosses did.

To my mind, the price tags were worth it. Not because I appreciated the intrinsic value of these items. But because of what they represented.

They signaled my capability to move with the big dogs. They qualified me to handle clients with considerably larger portfolios; deemed me worthy of further promotion. Yes, I had well and truly joined the rat race. All to the end of being more successful, affluent and prosperous. *No matter how misaligned I felt on the inside.*

Deep down, I knew this wasn't me. Don't get me wrong. To this day, I love being able to afford the finer things and adding to my list of achievements.

But back then, the intention and motives behind my actions weren't in-tune with my highest self. Rather than doing what was right for me, I did what was expected or what I thought was prosperous living.

At that stage, I hadn't realized the total cost — what I had to give up and endure for prosperity's sake. I hadn't asked myself if it was a price I was willing to pay.

It's easy to look at someone more affluent and think, "Oh, I wish I had what they have". But how often do you stop and consider what their wealth and power costs?

Titans of industry, world leaders, the rich and famous all trade something for their status. They sacrifice time with loved ones to build corporations. They endure public failure, judgment and extreme lack of privacy for their positions.

Your willingness to pay the price for prosperity depends on how aligned your endeavors are to your innate self. Your purpose and your why, is the counterweight to the sacrifices you make.

In my case, I was giving up too much. Gone was all sense of who I was on my own because I had no life outside of work. I *was* my career. It was my whole identity.

What I was doing was trying to be someone I thought I had to be, someone who fits into industry's and society's expectations. And it was weighing on me. I felt stuck, subconsciously blocked and far removed from my soul's mission.

Yes, the financial success was there. As were all the trademarks of wealth. But I had begun to realize prosperity wasn't only about money. At least, not for me. My definition was expanding to include the luxury of healthy, long-lasting relationships, strengthening self-care and the freedom to do what I loved.

Besides, my attitude towards money was all wrong. At the time, it felt like a limited resource. If someone else had it, I would have to go without. Instead of feeling liberated by my wealth, I was tied down — like a dragon, guarding her hoard, constantly worried and alert to losing it.

Your financial security is important. And by no means is money or its proliferation bad. But it shouldn't feel like a burden. A dragon caged by her riches is a dwarf of her true majesty.

It wasn't until fate intervened that I started to see how limiting my beliefs were. In March 2019, my employers decided to shut the division I worked in. This should have set the alarm bells blaring. Instead, I felt relieved. That alone was a glaring sign.

Following the path laid by others is all well and good unless, like me, you lose yourself along the way. You don't need to reinvent the wheel to find happiness and victory. However, your destination will always seem inadequate if your journey does not fulfill you.

So, I stepped off the beaten track. I gave myself time to rediscover who I was, the purpose and resolve that drove me, and the application of various modalities and tools that brought lasting joy. By listening to the guiding voice inside me, I redefined prosperity. It now included:

• gratitude for my current blessings.

• freedom from limiting beliefs (e.g. thinking of myself as unworthy or undeserving of reaching my highest goals).

- liberty to think expansively, create imaginatively, contribute value and uplift others.

- opportunities to earn my infinite worth, meaningfully and with grace.

- connection with open-minded individuals and entrepreneurs whose abundant mindsets could inspire and empower me.

This new definition helped clarify what really mattered to me. It showed me why I had been so dissatisfied before — my life had not been rewarding in the ways I needed it to be. No matter how far you get in the world, you will always feel like something is missing if you don't hit the goalposts that count.

That's why I encourage you to understand what prosperity means to you. Look deep within. Be brave and bold enough to set your own criteria, even if others don't get it.

With my new perspective, I saw where I needed to make changes:

1. I had to arm myself with the tools to improve how I saw myself. This meant learning to process emotions healthily; and releasing the hold of thoughts that kept me from manifesting the life I wanted.

To this end, I used an array of methods, including positive visualization and spiritual techniques. Some worked better than others. Nonetheless, what stuck with me most was how thoughts stem from one's subconscious. Therefore, to be all I could be, I had to first reprogram those deep-seated beliefs.

Emotional freedom techniques and hypnotherapy helped. But it was journalling that gave me the

best release. Through it, I explored and detangled the roots of problematic notions. It helped me reframe setbacks as an invitation to find a better path. I stopped being scared of negative thoughts and used them to uncover the parts I needed to heal.

It takes a lot of effort to build your awareness and resolve your internal battles. The results, though, are more than worthwhile. The ability to process your emotions with understanding and kindness leaves you with a greater sense of peace. And a mind at peace, free from the need for external validation, is a powerful instrument.

2. I had to develop a better relationship with money by relinquishing the suffocating worry that surrounded it.

Do you remember what you did with your very first paycheck? Most people excitedly spend it, trusting they can earn it back again.

That faith is freeing. Yet generally, the wealthier we become, the more tight-fisted we can be. Perhaps it's because we feel we have more to lose, further to fall from our lofty stature. But while you should always spend your money wisely, there is no need to think of it as finite.

The universe provides. And if you believe in yourself, in the value you have to share with the world, you will find endless possibilities to renew and replenish financial flow.

When I transformed my relationship with money, I saw that spending intentionally did not dilute my wealth. Instead, purchases that brought me joy, or supplemented self-investment, furthered and enriched my prosperity.

3. Finally, I needed to build something for myself. An outlet that allowed me to empower my purpose, connect and contribute in a meaningful way. That's why I started my own business, allowing the best parts of me to add value and support others.

It can be daunting to follow your heart, to do something different. The status quo always feels safer, and the fear of failure can paralyze you. However, growth comes through challenges. Why hold yourself back when you have a bounty of potential inside you? Aren't you a little bit curious as to what it can unleash? I know I am.

To this day, I still use the greetings my Mum taught me all those years ago. Except now, I'm more attuned to how truly expansive those wishes can be.

In your own quest for prosperity, I want you to have a clear understanding of what you seek. What does a prosperous life look like to you? Know your goal, so you follow the path that leads to it, even if everyone else takes a different route.

Gong Hei Fat Choy, dear reader. May you prosper in the ways that matter to you.

ABOUT THE AUTHOR

Jocelyn Chong is an Award Winning and #1 International Best-Selling Author. She is the CEO and Founder of Seed to Sequoia. After a 20 year successful career in the banking and finance world where she generated over $200 million in revenue, she quit corporate to pursue her true passion as a Certified Life & Business coach. Utilizing her MBA plus her background in high level sales, leadership and management, she has now worked with over 500 entrepreneurs and teaches them how to earn with ease, attract their dream clients, and create a life by design. Her mission is to help business leaders tap into their soul's calling and scale their business with feel good strategies & intuitive guidance. Jocelyn has been featured in Amazon, Thrive Global, Digital Journal, FOX, Ask.com, The Times and Finance News World.

Business Name : **Seed to Sequoia**

Website URL: www.jocelynchong.com.au

Instagram: @jocelynchong

Facebook : www.facebook.com/jocelyn.chong.9674

LinkedIn : www.linkedin.com/in/jocelynchong

Email : jocelyn@jocelynchong.com.au

6
KA KI LEE

PROSPERITY = ...

"Prosperity is not what you have but who you are" – Ka Ki Lee

WHEN THESE WORDS came through to me, it was profound. For weeks I was stuck, wondering what I was going to share in my chapter. My inspiration, download or whatever you want to call it, likes to come last minute, and as expected these words flowed through me less than a week before my chapter was due.

Initially, I thought I'd write about how I learned to make money effortlessly on the stock market, replaced my six-figure income and quit my job as a highly prestigious hospital pharmacist but it didn't feel right.

So when these words came to me, I knew I had to go to a deeper part of me. The part that has been hiding behind the pain of loss; loss of my identity, and with that money.

Most people equate prosperity to money but in the last five years, I have learned that it has very little to do with money itself.

Money comes when you ARE prosperity. Money is a tool and not the be-all-end-all. Once you understand that your perspective changes and you will start wondering why we, as a society, think working ourselves to exhaustion to make more money is even acceptable.

But how can you BE prosperity?

Well, let me tell you, in order to have prosperity on the outside you need to have prosperity on the inside. You need to BE prosperity.

I am prosperity.

You are prosperity.

We all are prosperity. But we have forgotten what that means because of all the noise.

The noise from our family, our friends, our work, our government, our community, our society and so the list goes on and on. The noise of the outside world drowns out the tiny little voice in our inside world that just wants to be seen, heard, felt, and loved.

MY LESSONS

I grew up in a stereotypical Chinese immigrant family. My parents owned a Chinese restaurant and we lived and breathed it. I loved it and hated it at the same time. I loved it because my dad was a classically trained Cantonese Chef who has worked as the head chef in some of the best 5 star restaurants in 5 star hotels in Hong Kong and Japan, so owning a restaurant meant we were able to eat amazing food ALL THE TIME. But I also hated it because as a teenager, you don't want to spend all your spare time helping out at the restaurant and miss out on going out with friends.

The thing that was certain was that my parents made up for lost time with us, with material goods and an annual holiday back to Hong Kong where we basically did and got everything we wanted.

The new Nintendo Gameboy,® sure!

A new computer, here you go!

The newest computer games, okay!

How about a Tamagotchi, let's go get it!

Money came easily because my parents gave it to me and my younger brothers whenever we wanted something, but subconsciously I was building stories about money that I didn't know would come and knock me out when I became an adult.

My main narrative?

I am safe and worthy only if I have money.

Prosperity = money

My dad taught me from a young age that to get ahead in life, I needed to learn to invest and own my own business (a pharmacy in my case). But did I listen to him? Not entirely. I did the studying, I learned about investing but I refused to own a business because I saw how hard my parents worked. I developed an allergy to becoming a business owner/entrepreneur even though I saw the success that my parents and family friends who owned their own businesses had. But I was not ready. I was working as a hospital pharmacist and earned a nice six-figure income without the long hours and stress so why would I sacrifice a good lifestyle for stress and exhaustion?

Leading up to my thirties I bought my first house, a car, graduated with my second University degree, got married, travelled, invested in more properties, and on the stock market. Life was good even though I ended up in a role where I worked long hours and was stressed and exhausted. The upside was that I was respected at work, in a respectable role, in my respectable profession and my family and friends all thought I was successful. Well, heck I thought I was successful because I had it all on the outside. I was worthy, I was enough, I felt safe because I was my definition of prosperity.

Prosperity = money + respectable career + material success + other people thinking I am successful

---

Kids arrived and I lost myself. I still had the money, the respectable career, the material success, and other people thinking I was successful but I was lost, exhausted, and empty. I started looking outside for answers, only to find that I needed to look inside for the answers. I went from a complete science and evidence-based person to someone who embraces intuition, the unseen, and spirituality. I started to understand that prosperity starts internally and then it spills out to the external. I realised that I was not defined by how much money I have, my career, material success, or other people's opinions. It was liberating yet scary at the same time and a continuous work in progress. Opportunities to do something different arose and the entrepreneur in me woke up. Little did I know that I still had a few lessons to learn about the be-all-end-all...money!

Prosperity = ?

All my life money came easily, or so I thought. I never worried about money. NEVER! Worrying about money was just not on my radar, until I started worrying.

I had tied my sense of self; my self-worth, my enough-ness, my safety and my security, to how much money I had in the bank. I was so used to having multiple six-figures in there, it was like a soothing lullaby every time I opened my bank account.

Now although I had lots of properties, it didn't mean that they were actually doing anything for my portfolio and one by one they had to go and there were losses. My bank account was starting to lose its magical soothing abilities.

I didn't realise how much attachment I had towards money until I kept losing it in different ways, without really trying, and each time I would go into a downward spiral of self-hatred and self-blame. I had lost my identity after having kids and found it again, but the loss of money brought out a being that was a force to be reckoned with. I felt worthless, I felt I wasn't good enough, I felt unsafe and insecure. The more she came out, the more I felt all those emotions and the more money I lost, it felt like a losing battle - until I remembered who I was.

I AM PROSPERITY.

It is moments like these that define you. That puts everything into perspective.

The rawness, the realness, the fear, the anger, the pain - everything came to the surface to be released.

It was an energetic vomit that came out from the depths of my being and once it was released; the calm, the gratitude and the clarity settled in. The loving presence of my soul and my guides offered me comfort and for me that was evidence that I had learned my lesson and passed the test.

I was finally able to see the prosperity and abundance I have in my life, instead of focusing on my bank balance. The gratitude I have for being able to open my eyes again without the fear barrier was freeing.

I learned that to BE prosperity, I needed to feel worthy, enough, safe and secure within me and not attach it to something external like money.

Once again, it was a realisation that self-love and soul alignment is the key.

Prosperity = self-love + soul alignment + abundance mindset

FINDING PROSPERITY WITHIN

If you were stripped bare of your titles, roles, material belongings, bank account balance and the opinion of others –

Who are you?

What are you?

How are you?

Most people go through life without ever finding out and it is usually too late when they realise that they never lived, because they were never awake during their lifetime. They were too busy honouring the demands and meeting up to the expectations of others.

Who are you?

This question helps to get to who you truly are. It is not your titles, roles or what other people think of you but who you are at your core, your values and beliefs and how you operate. Some of mine are:

I AM prosperity.

I AM abundance.

I AM wisdom.

I AM divine love.

I AM quantum health.

I AM nurture.

I AM joy.

I AM kindness.

What are you?

Instead of tying your self-worth to your job title, let's flip it so that your job title is just what you do because of who you are. Who you are, looks at your skills and the reasons why you do the jobs you do. Some of mine are:

I AM an artist.

I AM a healer.

I AM a storyteller.

I AM a listener.

I AM a teacher.

I AM a thinker.

I AM a problem solver.

I AM a creator.

Can you see the link between who I am and my titles of entrepreneur, podcaster, coach, healer, sharetrader?

How are you?

You may think that this is a strange question but it is a necessary question.

How do you feel having all the titles and opinions of others placed upon you to uphold? Is it suffocating? Ego stroking? Does it make you feel happy and successful?

How about when you are stripped bare of everything you were told you were, so that you don't need to live up to any demands or expectations anymore. How does that feel? Liberating? Scary? Maybe you feel lost?

Getting to the bottom of how you feel about yourself, allows you to become self-aware and begin the process of change.

Maybe you're thinking, Ka Ki, my material success and my bank balance is what defines me and it makes me happy, why would I even entertain the idea of losing it all, I'm not stupid, it ain't going to happen. And yes, maybe it won't happen but I'm not stupid, I'm rather savvy with my money and yet it still somehow happened to me.

Everything happens for a reason, you must learn the lessons to pass go.

Life is unpredictable and we're moving into an era where being inauthentic doesn't work anymore.

Being inauthentic doesn't align with prosperity.

Look at the world around you, old systems built on fear, manipulation and lack of transparency are falling apart by the day. If you are doing anything in your life whether it's business, relationships, friendships, your career – and you aren't honest about who, what and how you are – things will somehow crumble without you trying.

And if you're not honest with yourself, you will fall and depending on how much inner work you've done, will determine how fast or slow it'll take you to get back up after the fall.

So do the inner work now.

Love yourself so much that you accept every cell that makes you, YOU and start aligning with your soul because once you have those two things sorted, you'll realise that YOU ARE PROSPERITY, and your external world will reflect it back to you because...

Prosperity is not what you have but who you are.

ABOUT THE AUTHOR

Ka Ki Lee is the Creator of Unlimited Abundance Academy and the Host of The Awakened Feminine Podcast. She teaches busy women how to create money on the US stockmarket in less than 30 minutes per week regardless of market conditions. She is here to change the stockmarket landscape by bringing in intuition, feminine flow and a strategy and language that is easy to understand.

Ka Ki became inspired to teach the strategy, mindset, and energy tools she used to replace her six-figure income as a Hospital Pharmacist Manager because she knew first-hand how exhausting it was to exchange time for money and this was a perfect way for busy women to create money effortlessly in minimal time!

Ka Ki is also a #1 International best-selling author and has featured in numerous podcasts.

Ka Ki lives in Perth, Western Australia with her husband Terry and two daughters Evelyn and Madeleine.

Website: www.kakilee.com

Instagram: @abundancewithkakilee

Instagram: @heawakenedfemininepodcast

Facebook: www.facebook.com/abundancewithkakilee

LinkedIn: www.linkedin.com/in/kakilee

Email: hello@kakilee.com

Podcast: @theawakenedfemininepodcast

7

KERRI SCOTT

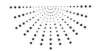

THE SOUL SELVES FRAMEWORK

"Money is often the perceived stumbling block that prevents our Ego from being totally satisfied with our present reality." – Mindy Crary

OUR EGOS ARE the very thoughts, beliefs, identities and stories we tell ourselves about who we are. When I ask myself, "Where do I feel unsupported by the universe?" The answer is often money. When I am not aware of aspects of my ego, I unconsciously give it the power to keep me from feeling joy in every moment. Yet, when I bring my awareness to my thoughts, I can achieve great love and prosperity in my life. According to Jon Kabat-Zinn, the definition of mindfulness is "Awareness that arises through paying attention, on purpose, in the present moment, non-judgmentally, in the service of self-understanding and wisdom."

The Soul Selves Framework is a mindfulness tool that originated from my search to better understand my soul or connection with source energy. I learned that how my ego interacts with me along my spiritual journey is an illusion.

Through ancient Hindu texts, psychology and modern-day spiritual teachings, I derived five Soul Self markers that represent various phases between the ego and the soul. They are the Bodily Self, Vital Self, Thinking Self, Observer Self and the Transcendent Self.

The Soul Selves Framework can be applied to every aspect of our lives. I first recognized this as I awakened on my grief journey. I had gone from being the victim of a traumatic loss to living in a space of unconditional self-love. Now that I understand the framework, I can easily apply it to relationships and parenting, food and adornment, and even health and prosperity. Each of our individual awakening experiences is unique, but there are certain thoughts, behaviors, actions and habits that are indicative of each phase of self-realization. It is our ability to recognize our feelings associated with what phase we are in that shifts us from reacting to life to creating our lives.

As we apply the Soul Selves Framework to wealth, prosperity and abundance, we first, find ourselves in the Bodily Self, firmly rooted in ego and lack. I know I have been here many times struggling with money. Here, we are not keenly aware of our thoughts and react to our desires with strong emotions. Money feels unsafe to have, earn and spend. We look to others to manage our money, provide for us or validate our purchases. Each purchase gives us sticker shock and our nervous system is in fight or flight. We are uncomfortable with our current monetary situation, the next bill we have to pay or regret previous purchases. We could be living paycheck to paycheck and carrying a lot of debt with no clarity about how to pay it off. We are worried about our financial future. Talking about money makes us extremely uncomfortable, so we avoid it. We are bored where we work, always wanting to be somewhere else and anticipating change. It is common to blame others for our lack and hardship. We say, "I need you to stop doing _____, then I will feel better."

A huge clue to recognizing the Bodily Self is that we feel like victims of money. There is never enough and we feel unworthy of wealth. This is our victim mindset. We don't have a clear understanding of how our past situations and limiting beliefs are guiding our current decision-making. When triggered by situations, people and circumstances in our lives, we throw a tantrum. Complaining, feeling miserable, resentful and sorry for ourselves are all actions that our ego justifies when we are unable to accept a situation, financial or otherwise.

Being in the Bodily Self is a good place to be as we return to it over and over again, experiencing the contrast and clarifying what we do want and what we don't want. This is where our desires originate.

Next, when we find ourselves in the Vital Self, we recognize that we have limiting beliefs around money. Thoughts like *I am not worthy, money doesn't grow on trees* or *wealthy people are greedy*, have been recurring themes in my life. But now I know they don't belong to me.

When I first heard "Money is energy," a possibility sparked in me. I craved a better understanding of money because I felt stressed about it all the time.

In the Vital Self, we desire to know more. We entertain the idea that there are better feeling thoughts available to us and we begin to take action to improve our financial situation. We set saving goals and begin to pay off our debts. Taking responsibility for our financial health is an important step.

Yet, despite this desire for change, we have a scarcity mindset. Our financial life becomes a series of things going wrong and our suffering and unhappiness increases. We could experience the loss of a person, job or simply fear a potential loss – whether real or imagined – and it threatens our ego. It feels like a real challenge to move forward or to know how to make a change. We are often frustrated. We say, "I want to feel better but nothing I am doing is working."

These experiences are created by our ego to protect us unnecessarily. We are beginning to unravel our Bodily Self and it projects fear that it is being lost. But instead of losing our ego, we are opening ourselves to our soul. Every time our ego flares up, it gives us another opportunity to name it, recognize its triggers and make peace with them.

Then, when we find ourselves in the Thinking Self, we learn to witness our thoughts and emotions around money, wealth and prosperity. We have begun to take responsibility for what happens to us, and our soul and the universe align to support us. We commit to personal empowerment and have a growth mindset.

Even though we don't have all the answers, we recognize that it feels good to celebrate our current financial wins and that celebrating attracts more wealth into our lives. We thrive on problem-solving, but we often get caught up dwelling on a situation. We get excited and overwhelmed easily by trying to improve our finances and we don't know what actions to take to fix our money problems.

I intentionally use the term 'investing' to adjust how I feel about spending money. This helps me take control over where I am spending and why. We often find ourselves struggling with thoughts of comparison, expectation and lack. When we catch ourselves in these thought cycles that make us uncomfortable, we say "I choose to feel better. Only I can make myself feel the way I do".

When we are in our Thinking Self, it is easy to dip in and out of our soul connection. Our mind will continually challenge our ability to be present in the moment and in our bodies, giving gratitude for our current employment, income and savings. Instead, we will wander off to thoughts of the past when money stress was dominant, or to the future, imagining ourselves with enormous wealth or suffering in debt. These thoughts will conjure up emotions with them that we give names such as hope, joy and anticipation, or anxiety and distress. But now that we are aware of these emotions, we have the choice to change the thoughts that do not serve the prosperous person we intend to be. Our awareness of our mood or attitude can be determined internally, and not by external events. We have a practice of checking in with our financial health and communicating about money is less challenging as we reap the rewards from the inner work we are doing. The great success is that we recognize how rarely we are in the present moment and that knowledge in and of itself is our soul connection, because we can remind ourselves to go back to it again and again.

As we find ourselves in the Observer Self, we are strengthening our connection with our soul and with source energy. We know our authentic self and can decide what is aligned with our purpose and energy. Ideas and opportunities arise for us to take aligned action where there is no resistance financially or energetically. Success is no longer attached only to wealth but includes our health, well-being, joy and satisfaction with the life we live. We know when we are fully present in the moment and when our focus has shifted away.

We are no longer bored, but instead, have a great amount of excitement and wonder as we work with passion and purpose. We are generous with our prosperity and seek out opportunities to support ourselves and others on their financial journey. We hold no judgment and are open and compassionate to everyone and every experience, craving the knowledge each moment holds for us. We release energetic blocks within us. We have accomplished awareness of our energy and can share our high vibration with others, raising their energy as well. We say, "I intend to continue to practice this high vibration and attract others to me with the same vibration."

Observing how my nervous system responds to various financial interactions educates me about what inner work I can still do. How do I feel when I pay for my groceries or hold large amounts of cash? Supported or anxious?

When I first had a thought that created an uplifting feeling about money, I took back control from my ego. The belief that money is here to support me, or as Francis Bacon said, "Money is a great servant but a bad master" transformed my relationship with money.

When we celebrate thoughts like this, we attract more thoughts like them to us. Then our inner well-being becomes reflected in the world around us. We have an abundance mindset. We gain the inner radiant experience and see that manifested in our lives. This is when we learn the most about ourselves, allowing our shadow self to emerge, reflected in every interaction, but safe in the love of our soul. All resistance becomes an opportunity for personal growth and expansion of our energy. We practice allowing and receiving with appreciation and gratitude. The momentum of our thoughts is working on our behalf.

Lastly, in the Transcendent Self, we are completely connected to our soul, our higher self and source energy, transcending our ego. We are blissful and radiant, completely in love with ourselves. Work is effortless and playful.

Even when we find ourselves back in our Bodily Self, we are no longer mad for being there because we embrace the contrast. We are powerful attractors, co-creators, and find harmony in this receptive mode. Our thoughts become things and we know the relationship between form and energy. We say, "I focus my awareness on the expansion of my energy."

We are aligned with everyone and everything we encounter, as they reflect our divine purpose back to us. Our connection with nature and the universe energizes us, and we sense the oneness of all things. We commune with the divine feminine, feeling inspiration, serenity and fulfillment. This prosperity mindset is to love ourselves unconditionally. Our full potential is realized.

It is my purpose to align with and celebrate this energy of overflow and return to it often.

Ultimately, it is the feelings we generate with our thoughts that are what propel our mindset shifts. The more we know, nurture, embrace and love our ego, the more we connect to our soul. The Soul Selves Framework encourages our self-awareness and is a guide to attune to wealth, prosperity, joy and abundance but it is up to us to embody the feelings they represent in the present moment and celebrate them. The first step we take is to recognize where we are a victim in our lives, then take incremental steps to feel better and better, more often.

Our beliefs can keep us stuck or unlock our infinite potential, challenge them often.

ABOUT THE AUTHOR

Kerri Scott is the founder of the Soul Selves Framework, helping individuals on an ascension path recognize themselves during their spiritual awakening.

A writer, designer, grief speaker, and thought leader, she is passionate about telling her story. Through her words, she creates a space for survivors of traumatic loss to be seen.

Kerri has lived the pain of losing a loved one to suicide after their diagnosis of bipolar disorder. Her grief journey has become her spiritual journey and from her loss, she has discovered the power of self-love.

Featured on numerous podcasts, including Happiness Happens and The Finder of Lost Things, she has also been a guest blogger for the International Bipolar Foundation as well as other publications.

Kerri is currently working on her debut, solo book, *Celebrate Your Grief, Transforming Your Loss into Self-Love.*

She lives on Vancouver Island, in Canada with her husband and their two children.

Website: www.kerriscott.com

Instagram: @i_am_kerri

Facebook: www.facebook.com/kerri.scott.39

Youtube: www.youtube.com/channel/UCEJ75278kZ15NEPYfrJLnsQ/featured

8

LISA LORNA BLAIR

DROMING INTO A PROSPEROUS HAVEN

"You will notice that those who speak most of *prosperity*, have it. Those who speak most of health, have it. Those who speak most of sickness, have it. Those who speak most of poverty, have it. It is LAW. It can be no other way. *The way you FEEL* is your point of attraction, and so, the Law of Attraction is most understood when you see yourself as a magnet getting more and more of the way you *FEEL*"

~ Excerpt from the Law of Attraction, The Basics of the Teachings of Abraham

Esther and Abraham Hicks

****

My chapter is dedicated to the loving memory of my beloved "Bonus Dad" David Edwin Barber (1939-2022) who prospered joyfully in passionate service to his Creator.

"Submit to God and be at peace with him; in this way **prosperity** *will come to you"*

~ Job 22:21

Droming into a prosperous haven

Fighting back the tears I pulled the screen back from the window and pushed the glass upwards, wiggled my head and shoulders through, braced myself on the sloping ledge with my hand, swung my legs through in a way that probably wasn't very ladylike nor elegant and then looked down.

Gulp. It suddenly seemed so much further than I had anticipated. The rear part of our house was higher than the front and my tiny bedroom was at the very back. Okay, I had made it this far and couldn't really go back, so it was time to complete the drop. And drop I did. Down into the grass cuttings and sandy ground beneath me.

Thankfully, I was saved by the flexibility and energy of my then eleven year old body and strong legs. I was down and I was on *terra firma*. Nothing was sprained or broken and I had made it out of the house and no one knew.

In all honesty, I hadn't really thought this through, I just wanted to get out of there, be away from everyone and everything.

My stepfather and mother arguing, my younger brother interrupting me, my older step-brother regularly abusing me and also spitefully reminding me that "our dad is not your dad".

I wanted to run away, or at least give them all a fright, make them miss me.

In short, since I was starved of attention, I was doing what I thought would create some. Alas, none of that happened! I walked down our street, took a left and headed to one of my favourite places, the riverfront. I wandered around, looked for tadpoles (a favourite pastime), skimmed some stones across the water and watched the sun descend in the sky.

Thankfully, my childhood occurred during an era where it was relatively safe to be out playing until dark. My "running away" plan was flawed. I hadn't even packed anything, so when I skulked back in through the front door, no one even knew I had left the house.

Looking back now I see the little girl who was bottling things up and yet inwardly screaming for attention. Feeling displaced, not truly belonging, just bobbing around like a cork at sea.

I look back now and realise I probably had not felt "at home" in this house since arriving there as a three-year-old when my mum got married. We were both yearning to be part of a family and living in a home we could call our own, and for 18 months it was probably like that. But after my younger brother was born and my older step brother moved in with us, it changed.

The marriage became unhappy and strained. When I was twelve my mother eventually took the courageous step to leave and the succession of regular house moves began. After initially landing at my grandpa's home we made regular shifts in and out of rentals (never quite daring to fully unpack and settle, as it was often likely another move would be coming)

I became a little adult quite quickly, but the three of us were happy and steadily "upgrading" with each move, whether to a nicer suburb or a slightly better home. My mother was doing the very best she could do, even if we couldn't put roots down for too long.

In my mid-twenties and pregnant with my first baby my then-husband laughed at how he had always been in the same family home and had only moved two to three times since turning eighteen.

We added up how many times I had changed addresses. I was stunned to discover that the tally was already over 30. (So, we had averaged a move almost every year of my life).

The phrase, "the home is where the heart is", holds such a great truth, because it's not traditional bricks and mortar that create this reality. However, the triggers of being displaced and having to uproot and relocate and start over embedded a belief within me.

And it was this:

I could never feel secure, or trust that it was safe to fully unpack and make a home my own. I just couldn't settle. My flight or fight instincts remained on alert.

After several home ownership experiences as a young bride and mum, a large home of our own was eventually designed and built to provide our three daughters a foundation and their sense of place. I selected tiles, paint and designs, and created the rooms needed for our little family. The girls could walk or ride to school and play in the park opposite with their friends.

A decade or so later this marriage ended. After selling off or giving away the remaining furniture and belongings and emptying the shed, the sad day arrived when I shut the front door on that family home forever. I turned the key in the lock for the last time and walked past the "SOLD" sign then sat alone in my car sobbing and screaming, the trauma all ignited. Yet again, I pushed the dream of owning a home to the farthest reaches of my heart and mind.

I neatly packed that idea away just like I had all my children's school photos, art works and photo albums. The beloved memories I cherished, the moments I adored, were all boxed up and suppressed.

Was I prosperous at this point? Was I thriving? Was I abundant?

It didn't feel so. Starting all over again in my mid-forties had NOT been part of my life plan!! Yet, I look back now at the abundance I DID HAVE – my health, my memories, my courage, resilience and the chance to write new chapters.

More than a decade later, it's almost surreal, but I am sitting in my beautiful home office, gazing out at a thriving abundant garden surrounded by tall trees with afternoon sunlight kissing their leaves. A delirious floral fragrance wafts in and my eye is momentarily caught by a large grasshopper scaling a vine. Birds are serenading me with evensong and the cool change in the air gently reminds me that Autumn is on its way.

This dream setting matches part of a vision I scripted just a few years prior. Almost exactly. Crystal clear images of a beautiful work-from-home space, filled with light and joy, being my own boss with the ability to set my own timetable – and be surrounded by nature, not an office cubicle.

There is much more to this property – dream acreage, rainforest, the exact number of living spaces and bedrooms, a home movie theatre, a work shed, veggie gardens, a swimming pool and all located in a beautiful little village atmosphere – I could go on.

But suffice to say, it manifested as designed. The powerful intentions, heartfelt prayers, the shared visions for this home are almost exactly what was created in our minds first.

In fact, in many ways it exceeded that. Is that surprising? Not at all. My soul mate Kevin and I simply requested the Creator to show us "This, or something better" – and that's exactly what appeared.

This energy of prosperity, this feeling of thriving, being alive and secure and being "HOME" was birthed from seeds sown many years prior and evolved from surrendering to the inner work and many lessons learned along the way.

When we first began our journey together we totally manifested the "wrong things" as we naively spoke those into reality. Many years of mentoring, coaching peeled back the layers of trauma, limiting beliefs and ingrained habits led to now. The more we surrendered and humbled ourselves, the more our prosperity codes unlocked.

Anything that no longer served was stripped away. Sometimes gently, sometimes brutally!

The earth was laid bare, new seeds were sown and we poured gratitude on them to help them flourish and grow.

Codes of prosperity began to emerge. The thriving began. And it joyfully continues!

Moving interstate and leaving our beloved family and dear friends behind was simultaneously our biggest challenge and our most exciting adventure, and after five years of renting and moving every twelve months…. finding a place to call our own was high on our agenda. When you understand the Universal Laws, you know well that the Law of Attraction does indeed magnetise things to us but the timing is not necessarily linear!

As a Manifestation Muse now coaching others with Gratitude and Abundance practices, let me gift you the rhyming phrase I share to help them amplify their manifestations:

> ***"Our job is to focus on the WHAT and the NOW, while the Universe takes care of the WHEN and the HOW"***

FYI: Feel free to insert whatever word feels most aligned for you – Universe/God/Creator/Source/Spirit/Higher Power/Source Energy/Higher Self. *(If you are triggered by some words and not others, please just focus on the one that is right FOR YOU)*

The **WHAT** – is the manifestation. What we desire to create, to see unfold.

The **NOW** – is living in this present moment. Stopping the chitter-chatter in our heads about the past, or the future, which only leads to anxiety and frustration. Be in the NOW. Meditate, ground yourself, find what you need to FEEL good right NOW, get into that vortex and live that truth. And regularly maintain gratitude, self-care and joy.

When we activate these things and we are in full trust and flow and surrender, then the Creator will magnetise the **WHEN** and the **HOW** to us.

Far too often we get stuck on the HOW and want to "fix it" and create the result, instead of allowing the miracle to MANIFEST. We put our expectations in the way of the "best and highest possible" solutions and then wonder why our version of prosperity doesn't appear!

I deserve, I allow, I receive

This saying doesn't just relate to money but to ALL iterations of prosperity and abundance.

Prosperity Codes are born from pure Source Energy – not from us – the FEELING is where the true magic happens. Money and material things are just one outward version of manifesting prosperity, but far greater is the way we FEEL and the way we GIVE.

Tune in to the Frequency of Gratitude and acknowledge ALL the prosperity you have already created in your life and how that makes you FEEL. Then, more will magnetise and appear!

How did we apply all this to creating our dream home? And what is DROMING?

We began with GRATITUDE – complete, uninhibited appreciation for ALL the homes through our lives. Thankfully we always had a roof over our heads, parents and step-parents and other loved ones who did the best they could with what they had learned or experienced.

Gratitude for the residences we shared since our marriage in 2015, each rental or purchased property showed us what we did – and did NOT desire – in our ideal dream home.

Then the FEELING. What feeling did we want to create and achieve? We focused on peace, tranquillity, ease and flow. For guests to feel welcome, as if they were at a retreat space, to enjoy natural light and flow and to have their own private guest wing.

We desired the beauty and energy of being nestled in nature – be it a sea change or a tree change. To have that abundant feeling of life around us and to feel total bliss arriving at our gate and drawn into a welcoming space filled with peace, love and energy.

To amplify the feeling, we then took action – we began DROMING. This is our curated word from combining two words – "Dream homing". Our week-ends were devoted to this practice with joyful energy. "Let's go droming!" we said with glee.

We didn't have the funds, we didn't have any approvals or even a deposit, so on the surface it looked impossible, but focused on the prosperous FEELING of a dream home.

The steps:

1. Pages in my Vision Book devoted to dream homes – images of properties that resonated with our desires, sourced from sales brochures, magazines and websites
2. On Saturdays we drove to as many "open home" viewings as possible. We talked to real estate agents, looked at houses we loved, houses that

helped us know what we did NOT want (!) and ignored the budget constraints.
3. On Sundays we visited charity prize homes and/or display homes and wandered through, taking short videos, photos, seeing ourselves living there, FEELING as if it were ours. Along the way, we were gathering ideas and preferences for colours, design styles and clever uses of light and shade to create cool and warm spaces.

DROMING was our guilty pleasure, our happy obsession. We would even add photos and videos to our social media and this became fun for our friends too, as they followed the "Droming" journey and added their enthusiasm and support to expand our vision.

Unwavering belief, trust and surrender combined with those action steps brought a prosperous result. Beliefs around money and receiving run DEEP – because it is CODED within us. This then defines and enables us and yes, until diving into the inner work, it also LIMITS us. The good news: We CAN change the coding, collapse time and heal. Ready? Let's unlock the prosperity codes, fully receive and bring them to life! It's time to shine!

ABOUT THE AUTHOR

Lisa Lorna Blair combines her love of the Law of Attraction, Gratitude and abundance with her passion for health, wellness and conscious living.

A former journalist, editor, radio broadcaster and PR manager, she now spends her days inspiring others as a Manifestation Muse, Gratitude Goddess, Financially Free Female, Conscious Online Entrepreneur, Coach, Mentor, Author, Queen of Positivity and High Vibes.

Lisa is also a proud wife, mum, young grandma, empath, ambivert and friend.

She is at her happiest at the beach, or amongst the nature and birdsong on the dream property she and her soulmate husband manifested in beautiful Queensland, Australia.

Alcohol-free since August 2019 and a heart warrior since June 2021 (valve surgery), she fuels her cells with plant-based foods and drinks high vibe, organic ceremonial cacao and alkalised, ionised 9.5pH water while continuing to manifest her life by design with her global online community of conscious entrepreneurs.

Website: www.manifestationmuse.me

Facebook group: www.facebook.com/groups/themanifestationmuse

Instagram: www.instagram.com/lisalornablair/

9

MARDALENA DAWN TURPEL

10 THINGS TO DO FOR A HAPPIER MARDALENA DAWN

I LIVE my days surrounded by males. The only thing close to female energy in our house, aside from my glorious self, comes from our kitty, Jaspar and our turtle, Lamigra. There are seven penises with varying degrees of accuracy aiming at my toilet. I am a forty-four year old, female head of a blended household full of five boys aged seven to fifteen years old. I am not used to talking about prosperity and abundance. I am not accustomed to explaining what these concepts mean to me or how or even if I manifest them in my life. But I absolutely consider myself an expert on actually doing it.

I have always been drawn to the energetic wavelengths or frequencies of prosperity long before I even knew such things existed. I remember thinking, very boldly for an eighteen year old, that I had tasted REAL happiness and if I couldn't sustain a life filled with such happiness, then I wasn't interested - plain and simple. From my perspective I was surrounded by adults who were unhappy and unfulfilled with their lives and I was terrified of facing the same fate. As a baby adult, I didn't understand the complexities that arise the more rotations around the sun we gather under our belts, but I naively and bravely didn't care. The "real" happiness I had tasted was my connection to the source, life energy, God, the multiverse. Whatever you call it, I had touched it and I wanted more. As we age we realize, life is not lived only in the high points.

The first time I became consciously aware of fighting my way through the heavy fog of depression was a few years before this revelation, when I was sixteen years old. I was working at the local movie theater and there was always downtime when the movies were playing and all the other tasks were complete. I remember standing behind the concession counter, wearing the ugly, itchy, maroon vest, gazing out of the floor to ceiling windows, over the rows of cars in the parking lot, feeling as gray and hopeless as the scene that lay before me. Let's be proactive and make a list for happiness, I thought. I found a piece of paper and wrote across the top:

10 things to do for a Happier Mardalena Dawn

It started off with small, achievable things like making and eating frozen grape juice or buying and drinking a Big Gulp of Pepsi. As a kid, I grew up on a farm in Colorado on 10 acres in the country, in a house we built ourselves while we lived there. We moved in when I was five years old and we had finished building the basement. We continued to build the top two floors over the next nine years while my brothers and I grew up. We grew and canned our own vegetables, raised chickens, ducks and turkeys for meat and eggs and were allowed little in the way of processed sugar. As a teenager with the freedom a paycheck and a car gave me, I found soda and fell in love. What can I say? It was cheap, available and would elevate my mood pretty quickly.

Further down my happiness list I started to imagine deeper steps I could take for a more lasting, grounded path to emotional stability, like spending more time with my friends, organizing my room, finally talking to Nick or kissing Sarah. The items on those first happiness lists were pretty childish, I was a child writing them. The act of writing the list was my healer soul showing herself and I am so grateful I embraced her at such a young age.

The first 'things to do' on my list helped me to embrace the power of baby steps. Doing what you can handle no matter how small, to begin to heal and head in the desired direction. This is ground zero, numero uno for me. The #1 thing to do for a happier Mardalena Dawn? Take baby steps in the desired direction. This led me to my next right step—celebrate your accomplishments no matter how big or how small. My best friend Rob Staggs, and I practiced this method of living in my early twenties. We ran around the world giving each other and ourselves all the acknowledgement and encouragement our little hearts desired. This was when I developed my deep foundation of self love and self forgiveness. The beginning of learning what true love meant. Meeting myself where I was, naked and unafraid of my darkest shadows, giving love to what I found when I shined a light there. Later in life I would forget this, when I let others' opinions or expectations override my self love. The foundation I built back then is always there for me to return to when I realize I have veered off my path. At times, I just had to dig a little deeper to find it.

Many years later I slipped into a postpartum depression after my second son was born. Burnt out from over giving in my massage practice and deeply struggling in my relationship with my husband, my 10 things to do for a happier Mardalena Dawn list looked quite different and was written with tears pouring down my face. There were many, many changes I needed to make. Motherhood had opened up a flood of insecurities and I had let them overtake me. I let fear over my boys' futures and insecurities about my ability to mother them, drive a wedge between me and my intuition. What was going to save me and shift me back towards a vibration of prosperity, was to learn to raise my standards and develop some boundaries.

Sh*t, even convincing myself that I deserved boundaries was a huge hurdle that took a crap ton of unlearning to clear. Much of my identity was based on the notion that strength comes from needing nothing and giving everything. This was the golden ideal on which to live. Reading that now, half of me is laughing at the absurdity of that belief, but a part of me can still feel the pull of my ancestors silently but steadfastly standing behind that statement. I want to hug them and give them a massage so they can release the belief that struggling equals honor and righteousness.

My paternal grandpa, Everett Hazen, used to say, "If you can dance all night, you can get up and work in the morning!" I love my grandpa so much and I embrace this polarity, work hard, play hard. I would have loved to have taken the chance to teach him to add REST hard. We need all three!

I began to give myself bigger breaks at work, thirty minutes between clients instead of the industry standard of fifteen minutes. I capped my work day at no more than five hours of massage per day. The funny thing I noticed? Nobody batted an eyelash. There was no reason for me to have this open spigot of my time and energy indiscriminately spraying all over my world. When I adapted boundaries and put a nozzle on my precious energy, I found I had some to call on when I needed it. I began to love my work again and as my energy reserves began to refill, my nervous system began to calm down and my postpartum depression subsided. I was more present with my babies and life in general became easier to live.

I had learned to develop and institute healthy boundaries at work, but I was not able to figure out how to fix my marriage. After my marriage fell apart and I was living as a single mother, I fell into a long period of scarcity. I didn't see the connection to how my behavior was leading me to this state. I saw myself as being protective, proactive, looking out for the future and planning ahead for every scary scenario I could imagine, while tossing and turning in my bed every night. Scanning the free lists, pinching my pennies, reusing, repurposing, couponing, saving for a rainy day, holding tightly, saying no, building fear. Not realizing it but steadily becoming very afraid. I thought I was temporarily surviving but I ended up slipping into a survival frequency that I lived in for way too long. My bank account began to shrink and it wasn't filling back up.

When you are in survival mode, a lot of compromises are made. Compromises to health, time, energy, dreams for the future and peace in the present. The tighter I held on to the fear and the less I gave to myself, my boys and those around me, the less and less I received. Even as I rebuilt the pieces of my life, a place to live, a new job, a car, I was unable to return to a state of abundance. I was unable to feel my connection to the source. My nervous system was shot. I was so mad at myself. What I saw as the mistakes I had made were so gross, so embarrassing, so hard to look at and accept much less love and forgive myself for, so I didn't. Of course, I couldn't accept responsibility for any of that consciously, so I started blaming everyone else for anything and everything that caused me a mild inconvenience or legitimate hardship.

My ex is a narcissistic, abusive, manipulator so co parenting is off the table and trying to implement consistent, healthy parenting is hard ALL THE TIME. My partner's ex doesn't like or acknowledge me, so parenting my step boys is impossible. My partner lets his ex control the parenting rules in our household. I can't be the Mom I want to be to my boys or my partner's boys because of all the outside forces. My partner is working on himself, how dare he? How dare he prioritize himself? Can't he see how hard and f*cked up life is? Why isn't he trying to help ME heal???

I looked at the world and all I saw was an endless list of what I needed and wanted so desperately and it all felt incredibly and inexplicably out of my reach.

Then I looked down at my hands, they were clenched so tightly, I realized they had been for quite some time. How could I expect to receive anything with my hands clenched so tightly? Slowly I opened them up and the fog began to lift.

How could I be mad at my partner for trying to heal his wounds when that was what I so desperately wanted to do? Why was I allowing my ex or my partner's ex to have any power over my relationships with our sons or the experiences we had together in our household? What made me think I could blame anyone for how I was showing up as a mom or stepmom? How did it become acceptable to blame my husband or anyone else for my refusal to heal myself?

I was ready to look at what was lurking in those dark shadows I had been hiding from and refusing to shine a light on. Deep breath, here I go.

I had to face the fact that at twenty-five I was so scared of creating a life of my own, that I married a man for stability, not love. I loved him as well, of course I did, but stability was the motivating factor and it planted a seed of distrust that we were never able to weed out. It brought out the worst in both of us.

When I did this, I gave up control of my decisions. This led me to doubt myself to the core. I had given up my power which caused me to hide my true self from the world, which rendered me unable to experience moments of real connection with anyone, which left me unable to form deep friendships, which left me terribly isolated and alone for far too many years, which left me incredibly susceptible to psychic attacks and manipulation. If you give a woman a crumb of self doubt, am I right?

The first time I woke up and began to look at this desolate existence I had made for myself, ten years had passed. As I looked across the vast distance I needed to travel to get from where I was to where I wanted to be, I defensively closed my eyes and went back to sleep. But now I was ready. I was ready to take the baby steps to begin, to head in the desired direction. It was time to make another list. This list would be a distillation of all the codes for prosperity that my lists for happiness over the years had taught me.

1. Create baby steps to gently begin to head in the desired direction.
2. Celebrate your accomplishments, no matter how big or small. Progress is beautiful!
3. Love yourself. All of yourself. Do it! Do it now!
4. Forgive yourself. No matter what you did or allowed to be done or for how long it lasted. Forgive yourself, you are the only one who can.
5. Normalize resting hard as part of the work hard, play hard paradigm.
6. Everyone deserves to develop and hold boundaries and standards in their personal and professional relationships. Everyone, even you.
7. The world will rise to meet your standards. It is ultimately only you who has the control to limit your experiences.
8. Recognize and enjoy the seasons of your life. They are all delicious. We are meant to experience them all.
9. You cannot receive anything if your hands are closed tight. Impoverished thinking only brings scarcity. You are only limited in what you receive by what you are willing to accept
10. Live in the moment. This is really the rug that ties the whole room together.

This is most deliciously experienced by me when I surrender to the present with my boys. I split custody with their father 50/50 so they live with each of us 50% of the time. When they are with me and they ask for my attention I give it to them, I don't ask for them to wait. They really only want a moment of my time and attention and then they move on. If I'm busy I'll explain what I'm doing and invite them to join me while we talk. We still have an hour of story time every night before school which usually turns into stories of their days. If they want to share a youtube video or meme with me, I give them my full, undivided attention and presence. This is in no way always easy, but it's important to me to respect their feelings and experiences while guiding them with love.

I give our boys the same gifts I give myself, unconditional love and unconditional forgiveness. They can trust me to never give up on them or let them give up on themselves. It took about four years of offering this as consistently as I could to earn the trust of my bonus sons. When I want any of our boys to do something they don't want to do, like clean their room, exercise or eat broccoli, there's a base of mutual respect and love running with an undercurrent of encouragement and understanding, behind the request and their response. They know that I love them and want them to be healthy, even if it tastes icky or feels uncomfortable in the moment.

Recreating the 10 things to do for a happier Mardalena Dawn list whenever I need to, keeps my heart, my intentions and my energetic frequencies attuned to health, wealth, prosperity and abundance.

My picture of prosperity may not be everyone's shade of lipstick but that's not really the point, is it? Like much in life, my manifestation of prosperity has been and continues to be uniquely created and crafted by me. Tailored to how I experience beauty, fulfillment, joy, wealth, abundance and my expressions of love. The universality of my story comes from the codes I've developed to unlock my path to prosperity. Codes that may sound childish at first but applied when needed, become the fibers in the beautiful tapestry of a prosperous life. Codes that I can and have used to put back the pieces of my soul, when I allowed the outside world to invade and degrade my power and I had trouble finding my inner light.

These codes, creating my lists and fulfilling them, have gently brought me back to my light and to a harmonious frequency of prosperity and abundance time and time again. I encourage you, dear reader, to develop your own list for a happier you. I wonder where playing with and prioritizing your happiness possibilities will lead you?

ABOUT THE AUTHOR

Mardalena Dawn Turpel is a Master Intuitive massage therapist, the owner and operator of Mardalena's Massage in San Ramon California and an award winning bestselling author. She specializes in Deep tissue and Neuro-muscular emotional release massage therapy. With her experience, knowledge and intuition, she works with her clients to bring relief from physical pain and release emotional trauma trapped in the tissues. She helps ease her clients into a relationship with their bodies from pain to pleasure. Mardalena has joyously spent her time practicing massage since 1999. She lives in Pleasanton Ca with her husband, their five boys and their cat, Jaspar.

Website: www.Mardalenadawn.com

10

MARY GOODEN

I AM A FOUNTAIN OF JOY & PROSPERITY

THE VERY FIRST time I heard myself say these exact words my entire body shivered! Oh the vibration of such a dynamic milestone.

How do you explain something so magical in a world of scarcity mindset?

Well...it goes a little something like this...

I LOVE Money! I always have. The most powerful example of freedom to a brown-eyed, eight year-old girl! Literally, if you have money you can do whatever the f*ck you want. I knew it, I watched the way money brought happiness and despair at every turn.

Entrepreneurship was woven into every fiber of my being. I searched for countless ways to make money. Selling lemonade, bake goods, babysitting, and house cleaning, anything to fill my piggy bank.

My mother was a small business owner. I can still feel her courage, excitement and commitment. I watched carefully how it changed the dynamic of her relationships and family life. She was a great mother and she went after everything she had eyes for. Crafts, pottery, plants, cooking, baking, and the list goes on.

I recognize this feeling as the need to identify as more than a mother - a hard working business owner - SUPERWOMAN! How else were we ever going to make an impact? Not everyone will understand, but being a mother and an entrepreneur is a "BIG" deal.

I was raised in a "middle class" home. I am the youngest of four brilliant and very different souls! My father, one of my many Angel guides, was traditional in a structured and loving way. I give him big props for my money mindset. Even though it was generated from a scarcity mindset, "pay attention to your money" are the words he ingrained within me on a deep level.

I started helping my mom at work around age ten, one of the many benefits of owning your own show. It was a great way to spend some time with her on the weekends and make some real money, a little candy store cash. LOL!

I secured my first "real job" when I was fifteen. I was a bus girl at a local restaurant and we received cash tips every night. YES! Another step in the direction toward my love of money and ultimate freedom! My work ethic was one of determination and high earning motivation.

I AM DOING THIS...

I zipped out of my hometown when I was seventeen, celebrating the $5,000 that had accumulated in my bank account. Anything is possible I declared and whatever you do... don't have children. Children cost money and require time, two things that I wanted all to myself. Don't get me wrong, I love my daughters to the moon, because I spent ten years doing "my thing".

By the age of twenty, I had assumed the titles Mrs., homeowner and business manager. My vision board said two things; The American Dream and Corporate Climber.

I was on the ride of my life with a gluttonous appetite for success. Remarkable success was serenaded by the mantra "Adapt and Overcome"! I loved all parts of being the courageous, determined, motivated wife, employee and friend that everyone could count on.

Day after day satisfaction became a luxury I couldn't afford. I was deeply dissatisfied and looking for grace. Pensacola Beach unlocked the door to a wild and magical journey. The invitation to spend a long weekend in Florida with my husband at the time, was a GODLY one. I spent several days combing the beach for a new life, a change of scenery and the subtlest feeling of satisfaction. I arrived home with an "open to receive attitude" and a full appreciation for what would happen next.

Eight weeks and one bad day later, I jumped ship. I resigned from my current position and headed to church. It was a bit dramatic for me to say the least. My courage meter hit an all-time high as my scarcity mindset took a backseat.

Scarcity mindset is the BELIEF that there will never be enough, resulting in feelings of fear, stress and anxiety. This is everything I wanted to release.

Leaving behind a Legacy!

That was the message at church on that miraculous morning. It was the ideal setup for contemplation, who am I doing this for anyway? I was anchored into the idea that I needed to work hard in this lifetime to prove my worth.

Sound familiar?

This is only a program and you can change your mindset anytime you wish.

I had to remove myself from the experience in order to see the light.

This light was super Bright!

Transformation and Truth

I spent the next eight years starting a family and learning to manage the intricacies of work-life balance. I had good days, bad days, and oh so sad days. I still had an insatiable desire to be all things. My hat closet was bursting at the seams.

Enough came as a panic attack that shook my entire being! Space and grace was the one idea I hadn't tried. I spent nights by the fireplace with my daughters contemplating our next adventure.

I remembered the guidance I had been hearing for years… "everything you need is already inside of you". My inner being was begging for life, "do what makes you happy", "follow your heart", "love yourself"!

By my calculation, I had spent twenty-two years holding space for my employers to make millions of dollars. It was time for a complete shape-shift!

You can only receive what you are willing to believe.

I believed in my God, myself and my mission.

I leaped into the unknown like a Phoenix rising.

The short and sweet version is what I will share here.

Crack me open, I am ready to live!

Divorce, custody, bitterness, disbelief, heartache, gratitude, generosity and joy all in that order. I have relentlessly taken a step toward everything I have ever dreamed of in this lifetime and attempted to hold onto it for dear life. What I have learned is, holding on requires a lot of energy and effort, which leaves little to no space for letting in.

I SURRENDER!

I released all programming related to my circumstances and societal expectations and created a new way that fit my desires.

I let life in and allowed myself to remember my soul mission. One day at a time, one experience at a time, and one mantra at a time. I created a practice of seeing only the gifts that existed in each circumstance. I let go of the idea that life was happening to me and chose to recognize that life is happening for me. Every day I connect to my higher consciousness, God and the Divine Mother.

Every experience is a gift to inspire another

It wasn't until I started writing in multi-author book projects that I truly realized the power within ME and the experience that was bestowed upon me. Being a witness to my life reminded me of who I am and what I came here to share. It allowed me to see how my actions created my outcomes and that I could choose to use them as a gift.

Joy and Prosperity are found in your courage, trust and commitment to embrace your journey as a gift.

Daily connection is the easiest way to an abundant life.

I have a daily practice of connecting to my divine self. I speak, I listen, and I open myself up to receive my gifts so that I may share them with the world.

I use all the teachings of my God, Yoga, Meditation, Breathwork, and Reiki to harmonize my being daily.

I practice being fully present in an all-encompassing way.

I choose to take inspired action toward ease and grace.

I choose to believe that my desires are valid, in fact my desires are the gifts that I have been asked to receive and share with the world.

I choose to believe that I am a fountain of joy and I lead from a positive energy, therefore everything I receive back is a vibrational match.

I choose to believe that I am a fountain of prosperity, trusting that all of my needs have already been met.

I acknowledge, accept, and align with the ineffable truth living in the deepest part of me, rather than being bound by hollow definitions and limited circumstances.

My teenage daughters are full of love and light and share that joy with their peers.

I aim to be the ripple effect, the very inspiration that I wish to see in the world.

My soul is completely aligned with limitless resources and opportunities and I say YES to every gift that my God shares with me.

I share the voices and victories of leaders, coaches, and visionaries all over the world through Divine Destiny Publishing.

I hold a loving and healing space for Soul Mastery, supporting those who are ready to surrender to joy and prosperity.

I support awakening heart's with soul-satisfying retreats in Sedona, Arizona.

I am wholeheartedly anchored into my soul's mission, and I wouldn't have it any other way.

I have nothing to lose and I give everything to love.

I remember who I came here to BE!

Make the Commitment

I invite you to create a daily practice of making the choice to live in your truth, your light and your purpose. The universe is here to guide you, love you and support your alignment with abundance.

What does a joyful and prosperous life look like for you?

How can you commit to taking inspired action toward this vision?

What do you believe to be true about yourself, your business and your mission?

Are you willing to believe wholeheartedly that everything you desire is available to you?

Do you trust that your inner knowing is always leading you toward your desire?

If you stop believing, you stop receiving.

There is no right or wrong, good or bad, it is all simply experience.

Choose to move toward what feels best for you and aligns with your vision of joy and prosperity.

Treat this journey the same as you would a new friendship, get excited about it, prepare for new adventures, surrender to the unknown and have fun!

Pick a mantra to help you eliminate distraction. A mantra encourages you to practice activation of free will, no longer ruled by the seeds of your mind. Practicing mantra will reduce the mental fluctuations of your mind quickly. If the mind is steady your body will follow. Here are few that I have used to embody joy and prosperity:

- "Everything I need is already within me"
- "I am open to receive my gifts and share them with the world"
- "I am present in this moment accepting who I am where I am"
- "I love myself, I trust myself, I am enough"
- "I am supported by infinite joy, happiness and abundance"
- "I create abundant opportunities for others"

Use your mantra as often as possible to bring yourself back to present moment awareness.

BE gentle with this practice!

Be willing to play, always be willing to play.

The timing depends on You!

Remember...

All you need to "DO" is Ask!?!

Open your heart, your mind and your soul to receive the gift of joy & prosperity.

Peace, Love & Blessings

ABOUT THE AUTHOR

Mary Gooden is CEO and founder of Divine Destiny Publishing and Soul Mastery Coaching. She believes that abundance thrives in your ability to remain aligned and authentic, which is a daily practice. Mary has studied and practiced Yoga, Meditation and Reiki Energy Harmonizing for almost twenty years. By taking an intuitive approach, she focuses on creating a space for clients to embody Soul-Mastery, a mentorship program that awakens you to your wholehearted mission. Mary supports conscious visionaries, leaders, coaches and entrepreneurs in becoming published authors by sharing their powerful message, story and mission on a global platform. She has contributed to six #1 International Bestselling titles, and is currently working on her contribution to a USA Today Bestselling series titled *The Younger Self Letters*. Divine Destiny publishing has created two #1 International Bestselling books the titled – *Aligned Leaders & Wholehearted Leaders*

Website: www.yogaetcboutte.com

Email: divinereikilove@yahoo.com

Facebook: www.facebook.com/mary.s.gooden

Facebook group: www.facebook.com/groups/divinedestinypublishingevents

Instagram: @mjgooden76

11

SARA GAROFALO

FROM ZERO TO ABUNDANT

THREE YEARS ago I was a stay-at-home mom with two kids under three, escaping an abusive relationship in a foreign country.

My soul was shattered into pieces and the life that I had built was crumbling down like a sandcastle under my feet. I didn't know my next step, I didn't have a plan, all I knew was that I had to leave. I knew I needed to provide all of us with a safer reality and the only thing pushing me to find the strength to build a better life, was the love for my kids. So I had no other choice but to leap into the unknown.

Why am I telling you this story? Isn't this book about manifesting abundance? Yes, indeed it is. I will be taking you through part of my personal journey and the shifts I made along the way to go from physically, emotionally, and spiritually broken, to alive, free, and abundant.

My hope is that when you read this, you realize that you are capable of much more than you can possibly imagine. You are capable of changing your own reality with the only power you have control of, which is your own energy, thoughts and actions.

What I also want you to understand is that the journey to prosperity is one of deep healing, trust, and surrender. It's a journey of quantum healing. So if you're ready for this, fasten your seat belt and hold on tight because you'll be taking your own leap into the unknown soon enough, and trust me it can get bumpy at times.

Now let me start by taking you back to the beginning of 2020. After being hurt, disappointed, and betrayed by my closest friends just a few months earlier, I then proceeded to get gut-punched by life when COVID-19 hit. It started with me having to close my massage practice, which meant I had no source of income. Because of that I was $500 short in rent, with a lawyer bill equivalent to buying a new car, two children to care for, no job, and no child/spousal support. I was pretty much about to face homelessness.

I was crying myself to sleep every night praying for an answer, a sign, someone to rescue me.

But every day it felt like I was losing friends, time with my kids, my personal belongings and my sense of hope.

For many of us it takes us hitting rock bottom before we decide to make any changes. And this was my rock bottom.

This was the time where I had to stare myself in the face and decide to take that leap of faith. Because I was determined not to let my life get any worse. And once I made that decision, it was like Gabby Bernstein herself whispered into my ears: "The Universe has your back".

Shortly after that, some friends loaned me money to pay my rent, I got a job babysitting and I was able to hire a business coach who ended up being critical to my growth and healing.

During one of our sessions, I was expressing how I was feeling frustrated and scared and overwhelmed by everything that goes into starting your own business. Fear of failure was a big thing for me and after I was finished venting, he looked at me and said in a blunt but loving way "Sara, if you want to build the life of your dreams, you need to start taking responsibility, stop playing the victim and get out of your own way."

I was very taken aback and definitely offended in the moment (the nerve he had basically calling me irresponsible), but this was exactly what I needed to hear to be able to start to accept the following truth:

"Life doesn't happen TO you, it happens FOR you."

Learning this lesson was a BIG step for me in creating a life of abundance. In order for you to manifest, it is important to understand that you are not the victim, you are the hero of your own story. You have to take responsibility for what happens in your life and make the choice to take control and respond, instead of reacting and looking to blame others.

Once I was able to accept this truth and stop playing the victim, I could see that there were places that I needed to heal and areas where I could love myself more.

So after giving it some thought, I decided the best way for me to start healing and showing myself more love was by creating a daily self-care practice that consisted of meditating, keeping a gratitude journal and developing a connection with nature.

Silencing my mind and connecting with myself every day allowed me to nurture my being from within and at the time I needed to feel nourished and be focused. I wanted to have a positive impact on my children's lives and become a successful entrepreneur, despite all of the traumas I had gone through. And in order to achieve those two goals, it was imperative that I reconnect with myself and become a vibrational match for what I desired.

Once I started to keep a gratitude journal and meditate, I stopped focusing on everything that was wrong in my life and started focusing on everything that was working out. It was when I started to appreciate and celebrate what I had that those things started to change, and I was able to attract what I wanted.

As I continued to develop my daily practice and started to see shifts happen, being the personal development junkie that I am, I wanted to dive in deeper. That's when I started digging into and working to shift my limiting beliefs.

Something I want to make a point of, when it comes to manifesting the life you want, is that the problem for many of us is how we are currently experiencing life isn't aligned with what we *want to be experiencing*, because of the limiting beliefs that we've developed. A limiting belief is any negative subconscious belief we hold about a certain concept or ourselves. Oftentimes we develop these beliefs during childhood and they can be anything from a fear of failing, to feelings of unworthiness, to fear of judgment, etc.

Identifying your limiting beliefs is a crucial step in manifesting the life you desire. When you can identify and work to shift your limiting beliefs, you can start to operate from that vibration of abundance and manifest things more quickly.

So how can you start to identify and shift your beliefs?

One practice you can start using is simply to pay attention to, and connect with your emotions. Here's a practice that I use to bring awareness to my emotions. Note: this may not be easy at first, it takes practice, so be gentle with yourself.

When a triggering situation comes up and you're feeling angry, frustrated, offended, disappointed, etc. here are 3 steps you can take to uncover the root of that emotion:

1. List out the sensations you are feeling. Don't judge them, simply write down what you're experiencing. This will help you connect with your emotions and your body.
2. Acknowledge the emotion by talking to it and accepting that it's there with a lesson to teach you.
3. Ask yourself a question like "what does this situation tell me about the core belief I have about myself?" or "Why am I really feeling this way?". Keep asking questions that help you get to the root of the emotion and thus the limiting belief about yourself that is holding you back.

So now that you've identified it, how do you shift it?

One way I like to shift these and release limiting beliefs is through a technique called RIM (Regenerating Images in Memory). It's a body-centered transformational technique that helps to rewire negative thoughts, feelings and memories by shifting our perception of what that experience was.

These sessions helped me heal many of my wounds. For example, I stopped attracting people and situations from my traumas and instead started attracting them from my worth. I gained so much from doing this work on myself that I've now integrated the RIM technique with my intuitive gifts to help women break patterns and shift their life from within. Healing beliefs and memories that no longer serve us is a key part of the manifestation process.

Once you're able to start shifting and releasing some of your limiting beliefs, you can also start to weave in practices that focus on aligning your body.

Body alignment is all about taking care of your physical body so your energy can flow through a clear vessel rather than your energy constantly being met with resistance (i.e. limiting beliefs, energetic blocks, etc.).

Your body is a sacred temple. It's the ultimate manifestation machine. Millions of new cells are growing every moment and responding directly to the environment you create. Here are some Universal truths you need to know when it comes to your body...

You are what you eat.

You are what you think.

You are what you feel.

The most important factor in aligning your body to the vibration of abundance, is your nutrition and relationship to your body.

What we eat is the fuel for our body, which is why it's important that we have a good relationship with food. Food that makes us feel good instead of always feeling guilty. For me, growing up, I did not have a good relationship with food. I tried all kinds of diets and food trends that ultimately never worked. It was only when I healed my relationship with food and shifted from a diet approach to an intuitive approach, that I realized how attached I was to pursuing thinness rather than pursuing happiness within myself. What I learned from years of my own struggles with food is that diets only treat symptoms, while a more intuitive mind-body type of approach treats the root cause. And that is why I decided to get into nutrition and do the work that I am doing now.

Through my own experience, I've learned that when you're in a diet mindset, you're more focused on rules around eating and exercise than you are on using your own internal intuition. This is the struggle that many of us face. This lack of connection between our body and intuition. Reclaiming that connection is the key to developing a healthy relationship with food and freeing yourself from the guilt and judgment that comes with dieting. Because a healthy body and an aligned body is a powerful body.

The second factor has to do with your relationship with your body, this includes the trauma that is often stored within your cells. When we experience trauma, our body remembers and stores it. Every time a wound is formed (and not healed), it creates a physical symptom, or an energetic pattern that will affect your daily life.

Have you ever wondered why you have chronic digestive issues? Why the same, toxic people keep coming back into your life? Why you're still trying to heal the same pattern you have been trying to break? When you don't take the time to heal the energetic wounds your body holds onto, you end up giving away your energy and your power. You're letting the wound run your life, instead of actively sealing it into a scar.

When we do body healing work, we are able to shift our energy away from what's hurting us and move it back into alignment with what is good for us.

When it comes down to it, manifesting is all about using your thoughts, feelings, and beliefs to bring something into your physical reality. What we think, feel, and believe is what we attract into our lives. When you do the healing work to align your soul and your authentic Self, you become at peace, with no need for approval or to convince or change anyone. When you live from this place of alignment of your mind, body, and soul, you are able to find the resolve and courage to manifest anything that you want.

The healing process is neither an easy journey nor a quick one, but it is a rewarding one. When you are able to heal and step into your alignment, it will truly shock you what you are able to manifest. So I will leave you with this friendly reminder to just focus on taking the next step that's in front of you and be gentle and loving toward yourself along the way. There's no way you can screw up because everything that happens, happens FOR you not TO you.

ABOUT THE AUTHOR

Sara Garofalo is a certified Intuitive Health and Life Coach, Certified Ayurveda Counselor, helping HSP women to get to the root cause of their weight gain and digestive issues, and break free from emotional pain through a mind-body-soul transformation.

Thankful to her Italian upbringing, Sara's healthy recipes carry the knowledge and taste of the original Italian cuisine, while her knowledge in Ayurveda brings a totally holistic approach to her coaching practice.

Sara's goal is to help women break unhealthy patterns and become more intuitive about their body through a sustainable holistic approach.

With her Intuitive Gifts and Healing sessions, Sara has been helping women heal from the deepest traumas and roadblocks stored in the body that are preventing women from becoming the healthiest version of themselves.

Website: www.loveholisticliving.com

IG: @love.holistic.living

TikTok: www.tiktok.com/@love.holistic.living?lang=it-IT

FB: www.facebook.com/loveholisticlivingslo

SHIRLEY JOFFE

THE HIGHEST VIBRATION OF PROSPERITY IS...

SITTING on my stunning local beach in South Australia with my family around me, living a juicy life. I really have to pinch myself that after 24 years of dreaming, I finally chose to follow my soul's calling and move across the world to start our new chapter.

What I love most, is that I get to live each day aligned with how my unique energy works (Personal Energetic Profile). And now that I have finally connected, embraced and embodied my Personal Energetic Profile, I've been able to create a life of more joy, purpose and abundance - a place where my health, family, business, finances and spirituality are all in flow, alignment and harmony.

Of course, this is my Personal Abundance Blueprint based on my definition of what abundance looks like; but this may not be yours.

I've been fortunate enough to uncover, unlock and unleash my own Abundance Blueprint and make it manifest but that's not always the case for everyone.

So, if you're reading these words, I invite you to explore what your true definition looks like, and as you create your own definition you're permitting other people to do the same.

It's easier said than done, but it can be done. If I can do it, you can.

Let me show you how this journey started for me.

My experience when I was young was that of feeling controlled, being told how I should behave, what I should think, how I should live and what success should look like. In other words, I was living according to someone else's definition. And even as a young child, this didn't sit well with me. The message that I got was that "when you have prosperity, you have power".

And, although really well-intentioned, many negative messages were sent to me about people with money. And on the other hand, Money was revered but to have it, you had to work really hard, without fun, fulfilment, and it was just about making it through life.

And this is exactly what happened with my father.

My father made good money for us through his own company, albeit, working sometimes seven days a week and coming home exhausted before starting again. It often saddens me to know that when he finally retired, he got very sick and passed away shortly after without really getting to enjoy the fruits of his labour.

This is why I'm so passionate about people having not just abundance, but joyful abundance.

My mother was a homemaker and took her role as a housewife to mean she must sacrifice her own hopes and dreams. There were clear, differentiated do's and don'ts for males and females, whether you were an adult or a child.

As a consequence, I felt stifled.

I was unable to explore my gifts, my passions, nor did I get the true opportunity and encouragement to discover what I wanted to do. Growing up, it was about appearances and cultural acceptance.

Fortunately, I was able to find my own way to create prosperity and claim my power back. This made me realise two things:

'money = power' and 'lots of money = freedom'

So, I made making money a priority and I got pretty good at it.

And right there and then, I elicited my first interim prosperity secret:

WILL + DESIRE + ACTION = MONEY

My drive for money, however, came at a great cost: In an attempt to create it, I worked myself to the ground and it was at the expense of my health and friends.

I didn't realize it then, but my powerful manifesting gifts and my magnetism were being opened, and my belief that I could easily attract and create money was super strong. My subconscious mind, however, tricked me into thinking I had to work hard to do it!

At the age of seventeen, as many older teens, I sought freedom and left home to go to university. To have a little luxury while I was there, I did what most students did in those days in the absence of loans, I worked and got three jobs.

Within the year, the jobs on top of my university workload were too much for me and I got really sick. I caught a virus that put me in bed with severe chronic fatigue, it took nine months to recover and although I stubbornly tried to repeat my year, I eventually realized that a degree in chemistry was not my passion.

I took a different route, trained as an aerobics instructor (while completing a Business Studies degree instead), and as I loved to dance as a child I was finally able to be free to do something that lit me up as well as earn well.

And there and then, I elicited my second interim prosperity secret:

PASSION + FUN + ACTION = MONEY

This secret taught me that I could truly love my work and when I was having fun, I attracted even more abundance to my life.

After two successful careers where I had built up to high five-figure salaries and while running a relatively successful hypnotherapy and NLP coaching business, I met my partner and we started a family.

At that point, I still didn't really know how my energy worked and I followed what society dictated was "right", to be a working mum as well as a full-time mum. After giving birth to my second child, I got extremely sick again through overwork and stress and spent a further two years in bed with even worse chronic fatigue and fibromyalgia. By the time I'd recovered, I was pregnant again with my third child.

Once I decided to go back to work, I got my "big break", I was offered a high six-figure salary job which should have been the pinnacle of my career journey. As I was deciding, every fibre of my being knew that it was the 'wrong' way for me, the call from my divine life's purpose was getting stronger and at that moment I knew this was a turning point.

I realized I wouldn't be living my purpose.

I would still be living through old programming in my mind and would repeat the same patterns of exhaustion, illness, stress and frustration until I got the lesson.

I finally concluded:

The seductive illusion of being at the top of my career with plenty of money just wasn't enough anymore. It just wasn't worth it.

So I took the brave decision to turn that job down and was determined to find another way.

I started the deeper healing for my soul and sought to understand what prosperity, wealth and abundance was for me.

I studied and trained in many modalities, healing, mindset etc and found multitudes of different ways and definitions of prosperity from the business world, healing world, religious texts and more....and everywhere there was a slightly different way to abundance and prosperity.

Once I felt I had a good foundation…

I LET GO and detached from the set methodologies.

I tuned into my own deep knowing to discover my own desires and fully connected with source energy.

And by going through my own journey of deep healing and rediscovery, my highly developed natural intuition and yet unclaimed psychic abilities, began to heighten even more than before.

As I was integrating all the different modalities in my way, I realized I had unlocked a whole new level of energy that I'd never experienced before. It felt like I'd tapped into the "one of a kind" essence that is me.

And I'm not surprised, because I was now operating within my own Personal Energetic Profile and it's no wonder that I was thriving, healing and transforming.

I started to release myself from limiting definitions, societal conditioning and beliefs around money, abundance, prosperity, fun, freedom and so much more.

I stepped into the realms of limitless possibility and noticed everyday miracles.

This brought me a sense of joy and peace daily.

And also money started to simply arrive in easeful and unexpected ways.

Finally, I was breathing more easily and going with the flow more.

Now, looking back I was able to decipher the thing that had made the biggest difference and created these incredible life shifts. It was the embodiment of my Personal Energetic Profile.

That's when my third interim prosperity secret was revealed to me:

JOY+ PURPOSE + ALIGNMENT = ABUNDANCE

And abundance is so much more than money, it's everything, and I decided that unless abundance comes with joy, it is incomplete.

I knew I had to find a way to share this message with the world.

The 'Joyful Abundance Blueprint' was called in.

The Joyful Abundance Blueprint is an approach, a set of three elements that allow me to guide and empower spiritually conscious female entrepreneurs to unlock and amplify their unique genius and natural intuitive powers, so they can unapologetically manifest abundance with ease, joy and flow all on their own terms.

There are 3 elements to The Joyful Abundance Blueprint:

Uncover is when your true self releases the lies and misconceptions that you've held about yourself throughout your past and opens your eyes to the limitless possibilities of what your life can look like when you fully claim your energy and desires.

Unlock is when you reclaim your power and unlock your mental and emotional freedom so you know your unique path to your life's purpose.

Unleash happens when you stop self-sabotaging and living from the societal stories that you have around money and abundance and unleash your unique manifesting powers and your money magnetism. This allows you to embody your Personal Energy Profile so you can create everything you desire with ease, joy and flow.

At every stage, I use my personal superpower, my natural and powerful intuition to help my clients explore and embody their Personal Energy Profile which is activated by 5 levels of transformational healing, an approach that is not only extremely powerful but also unique to me.

I believe that self-rediscovery is a journey and even by reading this you are embarking on that exploration.

And if you're looking for a starting point of how to begin or even continue your journey, maybe some of the experiences I've gone through could help you.

These beliefs/behaviours didn't work:

1. Working so hard that I didn't notice that my body was burning out and I wasn't being present in my life.
2. Assuming that success had to look a certain way.

3. Not listening to my intuition, making myself "wrong" and not being OK with me.
4. Assuming that working hard was the only way to bring in money.
5. Lastly, not questioning whether my beliefs were actually true or an illusion.

Through these experiences, I've learnt that:

1. We are all different, our energy functions uniquely. We have gifts that can't be compared or limited.
2. We can choose, design and create our personal success criteria without compromise or restriction.
3. We gain peace when we embody our true essence.
4. We can have fun along the way and get to define what that is for us.
5. We can be emotionally and mentally free, which brings us relief from pressure.
6. We are all natural magnetic manifestors, we just need to understand how powerful we are and tune in to what we desire, rather than what we lack.

So... for me the *Highest vibration of prosperity is ....Joyful Abundance.*

My biggest dream is to see more kindness, awareness and allowance in the world, and more people unlocking their unique infinite essence. To see people saying "no" to being controlled, struggling less and feeling truly alive.

And for my part, I know we are all connected by source energy. By living through my infinite essence and facilitating transformation, even for one other person, it can have a ripple effect that helps shift the planet into Joyful Abundance.

ABOUT THE AUTHOR

For the past 15 years, Shirley Joy Joffe has been a Master Healer, Teacher and Guide.

Being the Creator of The Joyful Abundance Blueprint, Shirley uses her signature approach to empower spiritually conscious female entrepreneurs to unlock and amplify their natural intuitive powers and talents, so they can unapologetically create wealth and abundance with ease, joy and flow all on their own terms.

Having had success-driven careers in fitness and corporate industries which resulted in burnout, her journey of rediscovery led her to realise, that we all have a unique code for creating abundance in our lives and when we do it our way, we get to experience true joy. Which is why she recently moved to Australia to live her dream life with her family.

She is passionate about spreading her message and shares her ideas in her talks such as "The Art and Science of Receiving Joyful Abundance".

Website: www.shirleyjoyjoffe.com

Facebook: www.facebook.com/shirleyjoyjoffe

Instagram: @shirleyjoyjoffe

Linkedin: www.linkedin.com/in/shirleyjoyjoffe

Youtube: www.youtube.com/channel/UCxsSuZrjrPJaLR8-4CepUVQ

TRACEY RAMPLING BROWN

THE SEEDS OF PROSPERITY

WHAT IF I told you that the seeds of prosperity were all around you, well within reach and just waiting for you to activate them? Your first response may be along the lines of scepticism and disbelief, and I don't blame you. I felt the same way.

It's hard to recognise and lean into prosperity when you're stuck in the seemingly endless void of lack and scarcity. A void where money bleeds out almost quicker than it can come in.

Your personal pattern of scarcity and scrambling to hold things together may be generational, or perhaps there was a point where you feel like your luck turned and everything crumbled into dust.

But even in the rubble, the seeds of prosperity are there. Lying dormant, quietly hidden until you're finally ready for them to take root.

I grew up believing that prosperity was the result of hard work. Really hard work. Backbreaking, exhausting hard work. I was never explicitly told this, I just knew it to be true. Looking back now I can see that part of it stems from my family history—while my parents brought us up to believe we were upper-middle class, our lineage was firmly rooted in working class and immigrant origins, albeit with a genteel flair.

The men in my family laboured hard to provide for their families, building names for themselves from nothing. The women supported by managing the children, the household and earning what they could to supplement the family 'fortune'. Family bonds were close, and extraordinarily tight. Everyone chipped in and played their part in sharing the load. Family was paramount.

Prosperity was measured in modest, albeit typical Australian means: owning the beach house (although 'shack' is probably a more accurate term), and the boat—nothing fancy, but something big enough for everyone—grandparents, aunts and uncles, and cousins—to pile into and spend a few glorious days together over the summer.

My parents tried to break the mold. My dad got a job in the airline industry and worked his way up from baggage handler to manager. We moved around a lot, and had the opportunity to travel overseas. The seeds of prosperity were sown.

We've all heard the phrase "fake it 'til you make it", but this idea implies a certain amount of inauthenticity in the projection of being something, or someone, that you're not. I prefer the way Amanda Frances framed it in her book *Rich as F*ck*, where she talked about leaning into the vibrational frequency of wealth and abundance in order to become an energetic match for it.

Looking back at experiences I've had throughout my life I discovered that the seeds of prosperity had unlocked a number of vibrational activations along the way.

The Luxury Acclimatisation Activation

Growing up in the airline industry gave me my first taste of luxury and the possibilities in life. Nice hotels, business and first class travel, domestic and overseas holidays, exclusive club lounges, tickets to concerts, shows, parties and events. There was an element of glamour, but it was underpinned by the knowledge that we were only there because of my dad's position, not because we could *afford* to be there.

When a slew of middle management redundancies were made in the mid '90s it all came crashing to a halt, and the energetic mismatch between where we were and the life we had become accustomed to had never been more clear. Even still, the luxury acclimatisation activation had begun. This activation continued to unfold for me, layer by layer, over the next 15 years.

Luxury acclimatisation is the process of learning to become comfortable in the world you want to be in, from the incremental upgrades you can make along the way, to exposing yourself to the kinds of people, places and experiences you desire.

I feel I should also point out that luxury, wealth and prosperity mean different things to different people—your definition of luxury may be more along the lines of high thread count sheets, wearing organic natural fibres, living sustainably and growing your own food—and that's okay, the principles of luxury activation and integration are the same.

It's not about faking your way into places, or giving *other people* the perception that you belong, it's about allowing yourself to embody how it feels and integrate it into the fibres of your being. The luxury acclimatisation activation is very much an internal process, even if it appears to be embodied in external and material ways.

After my dad left the airline industry when I was 15, he became part owner of a luxury and classic car dealership. During my first year of university, I took on the role of receptionist and car hire consultant within the business, which gave me access to an incredible variety of classic, prestige vehicles. Cars had never really been my thing—although they were VERY big in my family—but it was hard to deny the feeling that came with getting behind the wheel and feeling the power of a Porsche 911 or a Ferrari Mondial beneath your feet, or the stately luxury and elegance of a Rolls Royce Silver Shadow and a Jaguar XJ6.

My parents had also purchased "the worst house on the best street", and it was during this phase when they decided to demolish and rebuild something more befitting the redevelopment of the area: a dream home that we affectionately referred to as "the mansion".

A new layer of the luxury acclimatisation had been unlocked: the house; the cars. But once again, it all came crashing down spectacularly when the business folded and my parents were forced to sell everything including the house to pay back the company debts that dad's business partners had left him with.

The next stage of my luxury acclimatisation came a few years later when I got a job in the jewellery industry working for a prestigious chain jewellery store. I fell in love with Swiss watches, training as an ambassador for TAG Heuer and aspiring to become a "watch rep" so I could spend all day, every day, immersed in their deliciousness and teaching other salespeople to love them as much as I did. The pinnacle of my watch career came when I won an Omega watches sales incentive, where the prize was an all-expenses paid trip to the 2006 Commonwealth Games in Melbourne, Australia. Despite the fact that I was 7 months pregnant at the time, it was an absolutely incredible and magical trip, especially when Omega discovered that my cousin was competing in cycling   and arranged to swap all my tickets so I could attend his events—and watch him win the gold!

Working in the jewellery industry continued to up level my luxury acclimatisation when I returned to work several years later after my youngest started school. I started working for a manufacturing jeweller who designed, created and dealt in ultra-high-end luxury pieces, mainly featuring South Sea Pearls and coloured diamonds.

It felt effortless to acclimatise to the vibrational frequency of wealth and prosperity in a down-to-earth, family owned company with a company culture that inspired teamwork and made you feel like part of the family. They gave me the opportunity to multi-skill across different areas within the business.   I became the primary re-threader of all their pearl strand pieces, and travelled to Singapore to train as a Pearl Grader through the Gemological Institute of America (GIA).

The seeds of prosperity flourished there. We were encouraged to wear beautiful pieces of jewellery during our shifts—predominantly necklaces, pearl strands or earrings to give clients an idea of how the pieces would look on a person, rather than just on display.

On two occasions I also happened to be in the right place at the right time while we did some training when a wholesaler, or a supplier came to visit, and I was able to purchase some incredible Tahitian, white and gold South Sea pearl strands for my own personal collection.

They regularly held VIP client events and launches in store, sponsored charity events, and hosted exhibitions featuring a selection of their own creations alongside exclusive jewellery pieces from their overseas partners worth tens of millions of dollars.

It seemed surreal to be handling diamonds worth more than most people's homes on a daily basis, and because the showroom I was based in was located in the lobby of a hotel and casino complex, there were times when we literally counted out thousands of dollars in cash.

But despite how effortless it was to acclimatise to the frequency of wealth at work, there was a huge disconnect between my work life and the reality of my home life. My circle of friends were super down-to-earth and my local community attracted many alternative and "hippy" types whose focus was so far removed from the wealth and glamour in my job. By day I was an anti-glam mama who did the school runs, was team manager of the hockey team, and spent my Wednesday nights and weekends volunteering as a Cub Scout Leader. I also spent my weekends working for my mother-in-law at local farmers' markets selling natural, cold-pressed olive oil soap and body products that she made. It was frenetic, and chaotic, and I loved it just as much... but my worlds were so far from integrated that it was laughable.

Still, the luxury acclimatisation activation continued to unfold even in my "real" life. It showed up as incremental upgrades of small things that anchored in the *feeling* of luxury: buying specialty flavoured tea from my favourite store instead of just the stock standard supermarket brand; purchasing a TAG watch not just because it was a brand label watch, but because as a hands-on mama I wanted something virtually indestructible; purchasing the Thermomix I'd been coveting for years, because it made things quicker and easier when I was constantly on the go; upgrading my work wardrobe to an Australian owned and made brand and purchasing fewer, higher quality pieces I loved instead of splurging on the sales rack at Target and feeling frustrated by the lower quality and durability.

The important thing to understand here is that anchoring in prosperity is about finding the seeds and savouring them. Recognising that often less is more. It's surprisingly easy to mirror prosperity even when you aren't over-flowing with it—it all comes down to the way you anchor and reflect it.

The Mindset Recalibration Activation

Abundance and prosperity is always around you, but while you're stuck in the vibrational frequency of lack you're blind to the different sources you can tap into.

Imagine that abundance and prosperity are like a river with lots of little streams leading into it, each one representing a different opportunity or channel for it to enter your life. When those streams get blocked with debris— your negative thoughts, beliefs, and the obstacles and excuses that you make for your lack of ability to succeed—you choke off the flow of prosperity into the river.

Recalibrating your mindset is a rehabilitation project with many different layers. You'll need to wade into the stream and clear the rocks, stones, twigs and garbage out of the way, to unearth the shadows, pain, trauma and hurt that may be submerged below the surface. Like a detox, the work can be fatiguing and bring up icky feelings that will make you question why things are getting worse before they get better. But as you persist, the blockages clear and the source of your prosperity starts to flow again.

When we first arrived in Italy and I decided to launch my coaching business here, I struggled to transition from doing a tonne of free coaching calls to signing paid clients. My first mindset recalibration activation started while working with a business coach who helped me explore why I believed my clients' results were less impactful and significant, just because they hadn't paid for the session. Obviously I knew this wasn't true, but I'd been struggling with feeling like I wasn't a *legit* coach because a real coach would be raking it in like all the insta-coaches made out like they were, right?! Wrong.

Even though I wasn't making money at the time, I was working with amazing women and the feedback I was getting was positive. My confidence was growing in leaps and bounds, but it wasn't until I'd activated the mindset recalibration that I was able to recognise just how much abundance and success was around me—I'd been too focused on the pure, dollar value metrics of success.

Within weeks I'd announced that I was running a local event, and subsequently signed my first *paying* clients. And then the pandemic hit. If I hadn't already received this activation, I think it would have been enough to shake my confidence so badly that I'd have thrown in the towel. Instead, I was able to pivot straight into coaching online without missing a beat.

It was messy and haphazard AF, and I had a HUGE learning curve, but activating the mindset recalibration had shifted everything.

The thing about mindset recalibration is that you need to take a leap of faith and allow yourself to step out into the flow of the stream so that you can be carried into the river of prosperity, rather than playing it safe by paddling around at the edges.

I launched my first 5-day challenge with a six-day turnaround, followed by a beta-test of my group program. I was finally making money doing something I LOVED, and it felt so, so good. I was continuously evolving and uplevelling as my vibrational frequency rose, but just as I found myself at the edge of a new phase in my business I hit my upper limits hard.

The weight of the uncertainty and months upon months of hard lockdown restrictions had been chipping away at me without my realising it. It was only the strength of the framework I had in place and the mindset work I'd done that was holding me up. I felt hollowed out and empty, and my confidence wavered. I continued to show up and serve my clients, but I'd entered a cocoon phase where I also needed to slow down and do the inner work. A new layer of the mindset recalibration had begun.

I started working with the energy of the moon phases, and recognising that there were cycles within cycles—it was okay to take time each month to do the inner work rather than always being "on" and in the doing phase. It took time to embody and integrate this new way of being, but as 2021 began I found my own rhythm and flow, and was swept up in the current of prosperity and abundance. I started attracting my dream, soul clients, and I quadrupled my 2020 income.

My 2021 focus word was *illuminate* and I discovered so many seeds of prosperity as I shone a light on the shadow work that needed to be done. Looking at things from a different perspective became the key to unlocking and untangling the deep-seated hurt, pain, fear, trauma and resentment that had been trapped deep below the surface.

The Alignment Activation

As I mentioned earlier, the truth about prosperity is that it means different things to different people, and what's important is that you're activating YOUR prosperity code, not trying to follow someone else's. This is where the alignment activation comes in.

It took me a long time to realise and integrate the dichotomy between the polarity of the things I wanted, and for the most part it was because I hadn't discovered how to activate the alignment of my core self. As a multi-passionate and multipotentialite, part of this comes from having a seemingly disconnected and diverse range of skills and interests, which makes it hard to see the patterns and connecting threads from up close.

Another part of it comes from the misalignment between our beliefs about what's possible for us, especially as entrepreneurs. In my previous sales roles I'd had no problem selling $10,000 diamond rings, or achieving $50,000 monthly revenue targets, but when it came to running my own business I constantly questioned my ability to close the sale and bring money into my business.

The alignment activation works in concert with the mindset recalibration activation, because it involves reframing, remembering and realigning. It's about marrying together your core values and desires with the embodiment of your belief that it's not only possible, but also entirely achievable for you.

I needed to get out of my own way—and believe me, I used to wonder what on earth people meant when they said that—by focusing less on the micromanagement and planning of every small detail or step along the way, and allowing myself to simply feel into my intuition. Was this the right next step for me? Did it feel easy and effortless? Was it taking me closer towards my big vision? Was I making the decision out of fear or clarity?

Activating alignment was the most challenging for me because I needed to unlock the other activations before I was even open to accepting and embodying alignment. It's been pivotal, however, in opening up new opportunities for growth and prosperity in my life and business—bringing my programs together into a cohesive flow, enforcing better boundaries in my business and personal relationships, and magnetising my soul tribe of colleagues, mentors and clients that I've been able to collaborate with in new and exciting ways.

My focus word for 2022 is *prosperity*—completely coincidental, but beautifully serendipitous to the title of this book. If you take nothing else from my story, I hope that you'll be open to recognising the seeds of prosperity that are just waiting to take root in your own life, and allow them to blossom.

May you live long and prosper.

ABOUT THE AUTHOR

Tracey Rampling Brown is a Certified Moonologer™, Moon Manifestation Coach, and founder of the Moon Manifestation Academy. Her mission is to help astro-curious, multi-passionate women reconnect with their intuition, harness the energetics of the lunar cycles and rebalance their divine masculine and feminine energies so they can ditch the outdated, burnout business paradigms, embrace ease and flow, and succeed on their own terms.

Tracey supports her clients through monthly New and Full Moon circles, private readings, and coaching programs that help her clients become perfectly aligned to manifest their dreams and live vibrant, balanced, joy-filled lives they LOVE!

An Aussie girl at heart, Tracey lives in glorious Italy with her husband, two children, and a Bengal cat named Maple. She has been featured on Thrive Global, Elephant Journal, appeared on several podcasts, and delivered keynote summit presentations. A passionate writer and international best-selling author, *Prosperity Codes* is her fourth book.

Website: www.vibrantcoach.com

TRICIA MCKENNA

NO MATTER WHERE YOU ARE IN YOUR LIFE RIGHT NOW YOU TOO CAN EXPERIENCE PROSPERITY!

MY PARENTS WERE DIVORCED when I was conceived. My mom and dad chose to get back together after she found out she was pregnant with me. Eventually, they parted ways less than 2 years later.

The entrance of my soul into the world was dramatic and unexpected, to say the least. The running joke when I was a young girl was that I was the result of a pinhole in a condom!

By the way, this is a wonderful moment to encourage you to please, never tell your child they were not planned, even if it is true. Doing so can have long-lasting negative effects on your child's emotional and mental health and will deter them from feeling worthy.

Growing up, there were many seasons when our family got our food from local food banks and our mom was on food stamps. She was doing the best she could to take care of us three girls on her own. The compassion I hold in my heart for my mom runs deep. The tough decisions she made, to do what she felt was best for us, had built resilience in her that is very inspiring to those that know her. We lacked stability in our home growing up and experienced a lot of scarcity with resources. But mom always made sure we girls had fun and that we spent time in nature, where we could play, run, soak up the sun, and experience the abundance that nature provides. Mom did a good job, not letting her lack of money keep us from having adventures. Both my sisters started working at young ages and both moved away from home in their late teenage years to go off and do things their own way. My older sister pursued college right away and became a teacher, and my middle sister pursued college and became a nurse in her twenties

Being a teenager was lonely. I was the only child at home and my mom was working a lot. I became sick and at thirteen I ended up needing to have my left eye removed, which was a traumatic experience for my nervous system. It resulted in a severe lack of confidence, self-worth, and a lack of trust in others. The idea of prosperity was absent from all the trauma. After experiencing so many health problems, I decided to leave home at 16 which started my journey to self-sufficiency.

When I left home, I was receiving Social Security benefits from dad's VA benefits. With that money, I was able to live at a friend's house and work a part-time job while finishing high school. That money was available until I turned eighteen.

My first full-time job was at a shoe store, and after that, my son was born so I decided to work as a waitress. I had my first son when I was just eighteen years old. After the birth of my son, at about six weeks postpartum, something fierce ignited in me. This was the very first time I experienced this internal intelligence that exists in us all. Some might call it a conviction, I considered it to be the divinity. Suddenly the responsibility of me having to care for another human being brought out a deep desire in me to protect and provide for my son. I had this overwhelming feeling that everything we would ever need would be available for us, my only job was to go seek it.

I registered for college courses and was taking steps to improve our quality of life. Nine months later I found out another soul was entering earthside through my bodily temple and once again would be adding another human being to my life experience, that I would be responsible for. All the worry and fear crept back in about how I was going to provide for us.

I see now how birthing two children before the age of twenty was God's gift to me and was the first step in changing my mindset, from one of scarcity to one of abundance. I became a very resourceful woman for my boys, sometimes that included unconventional ways of doing things, but ultimately, I became really good at figuring things out. When my son's father left us with no financial support, I was four months pregnant. I was devastated, yet hopeful as a sense of ease came over me that I would not have to carry the weight of him and two children.

For a few years, I was working two jobs and still taking college credits in order to better myself and to give myself a better chance at not living a life of poverty for me and my sons.

With two babies under two, some things started to shift. I started going to church with the boys, and I accepted the Holy Spirit into my life. I also started a new job with a bank and started to learn about money and credit. I was so happy to know that I now had a salary-paid position, with health benefits 401(k), and some sort of financial stability for my boys and me. This job provided me with time and financial stability, allowing me to also continue taking college courses.

There was a span of six years when I was a single mom, working hard to provide a good life. For two of those six years, our church provided our little family with a Christmas because I was unable to buy a tree, gifts, and extra things for my boys. There were also times they helped us meet the rent. When my youngest was six years old I met my now-husband, Paul.

Paul was a single dad and owned his own home. He had a similar upbringing as me and like me had an internal desire to lift himself out of a state of poverty. Paul often shares how it took eight people to pay the bills when he was a kid. His internal intelligence kicked in when his first son was born. We had a lot in common and both had an internal desire to live prosocial lives.

The first thing Paul taught me about money was not to be afraid to spend my money. When we met I had a red Jeep that was run down and had a broken door from lack of deferred maintenance. Paul got me to think about money differently when he told me, "You should never be scared to fix your car because your car is the tool that allows you to make more money", without a car how would I get to work? He assured me there was always more money out there for me to go get. This expanded my thinking and helped me feel free to spend money.

The thoughts I developed as a single mom had served me well, but if Paul and I were going to do the things we desired to do together, things needed to change with how I made money and how I spent money.

Shortly after moving in with Paul, I decided to become an entrepreneur and get my Arizona Real Estate license. The ideas and principles about prosperity continued to evolve. As a new agent, I was reading books, attending work-shops, and listening to podcasts to learn more about sales.

At this time some of the old worries were falling away while others crept in. There was no more worry about getting the kids ready for school before I had to go to work, or who was going to drop them off at school. No more worrying about who is going to take care of them if one of them was sick, or who would be home for them when they got home. Our needs in that area of life would be taken care of by me. Removing those worries freed up an energetic space for me to focus on other things, but the fear of how I was going to make money still existed in me.

The freedom of time allowed me to decide how I spent my time and was a good lesson on conscious discipline. I felt very prosperous with how much time I could be available for my family, compared to the amount of time spent working to make money. Even though I was not making a lot of money yet, the feelings of being prosperous were guiding me.

Then a new struggle arrived. How do I manage the large amounts of money I received at one time, how can we make it last? There have been times when I made $20,000 in a single month, which is a lot more money, way more money than I used to make in a year as a waitress. There was a long-running pattern where I became aware of where I would receive thousands of dollars and within a month or two it would all be gone. This cycle repeated itself for ten-plus years.

It wasn't until the last couple of years when I started my daily spiritual practice, that I have become a better steward of my resources. I took the wisdom Paul shared about learning to be okay spending my money and invested in financial coaching, courses, and mentorship. My spiritual practice led me to kundalini yoga and meditation. It is there that I learned more about money being energy and when we attune our energy towards the frequency of money, money will flow more easily to us. There are several ancient texts available to all of us that can help us learn more about these ancient principles, and I started reading them and studying them.

Next came my willingness to try them out. In 2019 I had a transformative shift in my aura, a deep overwhelming feeling about prosperity. Prosperity isn't just about having lots of money. Prosperity for me felt like freedom. A major shift in my aura and radiant body had occurred and the thought stream about what living a prosperous life looks like for me changed drastically.

Prior to this shift of perspective, I had what most would consider a prosperous life. My husband and I owned a home in one of the safest cities in America. We traveled a lot, our boys attended one of the best school districts in the state of Arizona, we ate at nice restaurants, had the big truck, camper, and brand new car, etc. We both owned our own businesses, so we had more time and freedom than most of our family. Even with all of these successes, I still was not feeling prosperous, I was feeling like a hungry ghost.

So what changed, how I did tap into the codes of prosperity?

It started to change when I decided to change the way I show up for myself. Following that, there was a financial and health mastermind at our office and a financial planner came and shared how rich people spend their money and time versus how poor people spend their money and time. It really resonated deep into my nervous system, and I experienced a rush of energy going through my body, like the one I felt after my son was born. Then I got chills when I heard the gentleman explain the purpose of saving money is so we can take advantage of future opportunities and not think about saving money in preparation for emergencies.

After this workshop, I asked my higher power to help me with my thoughts around money and to help me be a better steward of the money I was receiving. I started to make time for myself every day, where I meditated and prayed. I studied and read books on prosperity. I did forty meditation practices on prosperity, and I started practicing some of the financial principles found in the ancient texts about being a good steward of money. Additionally, I practiced having fun with money, and to me, once we can have fun with money you are met with an overwhelming sense of freedom.

I have learned money is a currency, and as a frequency of energy, when we tap into the flow of that currency - anything is possible. I can now live my days not thinking about how I am going to get money. I can live in the present moment and trust all my needs will be met. The freedom from fear of where my money is coming from is Prosperity to me. I hope to share my experience about prosperity with you, helps you to have hope and the courage to develop the principles and energetic aura to be able to experience prosperity too. After all, prosperity is your birthright!

With Love,

Tricia Mckenna - A Heart Grounded

Actionable steps you can take today towards entering the frequency of prosperity.

Set aside a minimum of 30 minutes a day to get a better perspective of your life. When you take time for yourself, you're sending a signal to the universe that you matter.

Practice having a daily gratitude ritual where you write down what you are grateful for and how God provided for you. It could be someone who offered to buy you lunch, a refund check you got in the mail, any little unexpected blessing you receive, write it down.

Pay yourself first by first setting aside a percentage of all incoming money away for future opportunities. Start with 1% and work your way up from there.

Pray a blessing over the money leaving your possession and ask God to multiply it. I like to play mantras and have a dance party when paying my bills. Any chance I get to pay my bills is a blessing.

Practice thanking God for everything you have right now.

Practice Kundalini Prosperity meditations for a minimum of 3 minutes a day up to 11 minutes.

Remind yourself every day that money comes to you easily and effortlessly and that you are worthy of a prosperous life.

ABOUT THE AUTHOR

Tricia McKenna is an Arizona Real Estate Broker, the creator of "A Heart Grounded" Movement, Kundalini Yoga Teacher, and an International Best-Selling Author.

Tricia offers Mentoring Services to people looking to change their daily habits and offers heart-centered Real Estate Services throughout the state of Arizona.

In 2014 Tricia was a recipient of the Top 40 under 40 Award from Young Professional Network for Realtors.

Driven by her own journey, she is focused on empowering others to achieve their dreams, get unstuck, break destructive habits and patterns of their lives so they can experience financial freedom, self-expression, joy, and abundance.

Whether it's personal, business, or financial aspects of your life, Tricia incorporates birth charts, Kundalini yogic science, mediation, and energetic practices to help you achieve your dreams.

Tricia currently resides in Arizona with her husband Paul and her Dog Rhea. She is a proud mom, wife, daughter, sister, and entrepreneur.

Schedule a discovery call with her today!

Website: www.aheartgrounded.com

ABOUT EXALTED PUBLISHING HOUSE

EXALTED Publishing House produces books that move hearts and minds.

We are an *indie book publisher* for leaders, CEOS, entrepreneurs, business owners and organizations who want to get more eyes on their stories.

Founded by Bridget Aileen Sicsko in 2020, Exalted Publishing House has a simple philosophy: change the world through words. Our aim is to work with a small number of entrepreneurs, organizations and businesses each year to uphold the highest standard of intimacy and personalization in the cathartic writing and publishing process. We mainly work in the realms of the alternative, disenfranchised & different by sharing stories that aren't always spoken through mainstream channels.

Corporate Books

We create multi-author books for business owners, CEOS and organizations to highlight the stories of their mission, brand, teams and employees.

Multi-Author Books & Visibility Projects

We work with leaders and entrepreneurs who want to get featured in top tier publications and podcasts and share their story to elevate their brand.

If you would like to purchase a 100+ bulk order of any of our books for schools, organiza-tions, teams, book clubs at a discounted rate, please contact <u>bridget@bridgetaileen.com</u> for details and prices.

Others Books by Exalted Publishing House

Legacy Speaks, Powerhouse Women Leading Lives Worth Remembering

Success Codes, Secrets To Success You Weren't Taught In School

Lineage Speaks, Women Who Carry The Torch For Future Generations

Where Social Work Can Lead You, Journeys into, around and even out of social work

Divinity Speaks: Women Who Tune In & Trust Divine Inspiration

Heart-Centered Leadership: Unique Pathways, Approaches and Strategies to Soul-Aligned Success

Manufactured by Amazon.ca
Bolton, ON

25678359R00072